QUIET WEEK-END

A Comedy in Three Acts

by

ESTHER McCRACKEN

SAMUEL FRENCH

LONDON

NEW YORK   TORONTO   SYDNEY   HOLLYWOOD

QUIET WEEK-END

Produced on July 7th, 1941, at the Theatre Royal, Newcastle, and subsequently played at Wyndham's Theatre, London, with the following cast of characters :

SAM PECKER (occasional Handyman) . . .	*Basil Mitchell.*
MARY JARROW	*Gladys Boot.*
MIRANDA BUTE	*Glynis Johns.*
SALLY SPENDER (fourteen-year-old Hoyden) . .	*Gabrielle Blunt.*
MILDRED ROYD	*Marjorie Fielding*
ARTHUR ROYD	*George Thorpe.*
BELLA HITCHINS (Maid with the ROYDS for years) .	*Helene Burls.*
MARCIA BRENT (the ROYDS' married Daughter) .	*Gwynne Whitby.*
ADRIAN BARASFORD	*Frank Cellier.*
JIM BRENT (MARCIA'S Husband)	*Geoffrey Denys.*
ELLA SPENDER (SALLY'S Mother)	*Dorothy Batley.*
DENYS ROYD (the ROYDS' Son)	*Michael Wilding.*
ROWENA MARRIOTT	*Jeanne Stuart.*

SYNOPSIS OF SCENES

ACT I

SCENE.—The living-room of the Royds' cottage in Throppleton. A Friday afternoon in September.

ACT II

SCENE 1.—The same as Act I, Saturday afternoon.
SCENE 2.—The same, about six hours later.

ACT III

SCENE.—The same as Acts I and II. Sunday afternoon.

QUIET WEEK-END

Produced on ... at the ... the Theatre Royal, Newcastle, and subsequently played at Wyndham's Theatre, London, with the following cast of characters:

QUIET WEEK-END

ACT I

The SCENE *is the sitting-room of a country cottage in the village of Throppleton.*

(See the Ground Plan and Photograph at the end of the book.)
It is a pleasant room, with furniture obviously collected from attics and relatives.

Back C. *is a deep bay, on a higher level than the rest of the room, and reached by two steps flanked by pillars. The bay windows have window seats. Beyond is the garden. On the* L. *of the windows is a french window, referred to in the script as the " garden door."*

On the L., *in the room proper, is a door leading to the passage which is also on a higher level. To mitigate the inconvenience of this, a hand-painted notice hangs over the door which reads :*
" Mind the Step." The fire is R. *In front of it, a large settee. Above it, an armchair. Below it, against the wall, is a windsor chair. There is a table at* C., *and another armchair* L.C. *Below the door to the passage* L. *is a Dutch dresser. Other chairs, occasional tables, etc., are depicted on the plan and set out in the Furniture Plot.*

When the CURTAIN *rises the fire is smoking badly, and* SAM PECKER, *occasional handyman, is kneeling before it, holding up a sheet of newspaper in the hope of thus inducing it to burn. He is idly reading the racing news upside down, and humming and coughing.*

SAM. " I want to ask you a personal question, Aubrey dear. I'm afraid it's an awfully personal question, Aubrey dear." *(Peeping behind the paper.)* Drat the thing ! Draw, can't you ! *(He replaces the paper.)*

*(*MARY JARROW, *a good-looking woman of elastic middle-age, walks up the garden path and enters at the garden door.)*

MARY *(looks around)*. Good afternoon, Pecker. They haven't arrived yet ?
SAM *(startled)*. Good afternoon, m'm. They're about due, but they 'aven't arrived—and thank goodness ! The fire'll not draw and I'm not 'alf done yet. This only came by the afternoon post this week. *(He pulls a letter out of his pocket and rises.)* " Light fires, dig potatoes, chop wood, open windows, if no lettuce, buy some."
MARY *(to him)*. And what have you done ?
SAM. Lit fires—chopped *some* of the wood and opened the

5

windows. The lettuce 'as gone to seed. It'll 'ave to be " if not, buy some."

MARY. I'll get it for you. I'm going down to the shop and I'll call in with it on my way back.

(*She goes out through the garden door.*)

SAM (*singing again*). " I want to ask you a personal question, Aubrey dear . . ." (*etc.*)

(*He hums, then leans down and blows under the newspaper.* SALLY SPENDER *appears from* R., *an untidy plump child of about fourteen, and clambers in at the window up* C.)

SALLY (*in a hissing whisper*). Sam !

SAM (*jumping and turning*). Lord ! Oh, Miss Sally, can't you ever come in at a door ?

SALLY. Not if I can help it. (*Coming down* C., *on* SAM'S L.) Where are the Royds ?

SAM. Not 'ere yet.

SALLY. Bother. I hoped they'd ask me to supper.

SAM. Don't they ever feed you at 'ome ?

SALLY. Not properly.

SAM. You wouldn't like to chop some sticks as your good deed for the day ?

SALLY. No thanks. I've done my good deed already.

SAM (*disbelievingly*). Wot ?

SALLY (*gloomily*). Promised I'd wear the frightful dress Mother's made me for the concert to-morrow. Don't laugh— I'm doing a dance.

SAM. I 'ope that stage'll stand it.

SALLY. I wish I thought it wouldn't. (*She turns up to the garden door.*)

SAM (*removing the newspaper*). Well, that'll just 'ave to do. (*Fishing the letter out of his pocket, he rises.*)

(SALLY *has wandered out of the garden door.*)

(*Muttering.*) Sticks, winders, lettuce. . . .

SALLY (*outside, but in sight*). Here they are ! (*Entering.*) They've arrived ! (*She comes down* C., *below the steps.*)

(*A horn tootles cheerfully.*)

SAM (*moving towards* SALLY). Tomatoes ! Gawd ! I never saw tomatoes. I'll catch it ! 'Ere ! (*Producing some coins from his pocket.*) Slip round to Jacko's, Miss Sally——

SALLY. No !

SAM (*pushing her* L.). Ah, go on ! Quick—and I'll take you fishin' next week.

SALLY. Promise ?

SAM. Promise, but look slippy, there's a good girl. One pound of tomatoes.

SALLY (*turning to go*). I'm everybody's slave. (*She stumbles up against the pillar.*) Blast!

(*She runs up and exits into the garden. SAM hastily folds the paper, sweeps up the hearth, gives a last blow to the fire, and looks round as MILDRED'S and ARTHUR'S voices are heard in the hall. He then goes up quickly and exits into the garden.*)

MILDRED (*off* L.). Well, here we are! Marcia, be sure you carry that the right way up!

(MILDRED ROYD, *cheerful and bustling, enters at the door* L., *laden with parcels.*)

Mind the step.

(*Her husband,* ARTHUR ROYD, *follows her with further parcels under his arm and tenderly feeling a fishing-rod in its case.*)

ARTHUR (*automatically*). Mind the step. I put it in the back most carefully and someone had flung a great suitcase on top of it.

MILDRED (*by the table* C.). Arthur dear, you can't *know* they flung it—and it's all right, isn't it?

ARTHUR (*reluctantly*). If it is, it's more good luck than good management.

MILDRED (*busy with the parcels*). Of course it's all right. Now don't let's start with any unpleasantness. Give me those. (*Taking the parcels.*) Where's the—oh, there it is. Oh, Arthur! —that was a gingerbread and look at it! (*Showing a parcel.*)

ARTHUR (*to* L.). How was I to know what it was?

MILDRED. I said " be careful "! Never mind, I suppose it'll taste just the same whatever shape it is. (*Going up to the window* C.)

(ARTHUR *sits in the armchair* L.)

Oh, isn't it lovely to be here! Hurry up and retire, Arthur, and when Denys marries or goes off we'll come back permanently.

ARTHUR (*drawing out his rod and carefully examining each section*). I'm not living here permanently with the present plumbing.

MILDRED. You must earn enough to have that put right first. In the meantime the week-ends are better than nothing. Isn't it quiet and peaceful! (*She looks out over the garden.*)

(*A babel of voices and thumping sounds from the hall:* " It's stuck!"—" You're pushing it the wrong way!"—" You try, then."—" Ease it at the bottom." (*etc., etc.*)

(BELLA *enters* L. *and makes for the garden door.*)

BELLA. The kitchen door's stuck again. I'll 'ave a go at it from the other side.

(*She goes out through the garden door.*)

MILDRED (*coming down* C.). We *must* get a bit shaved off. Where's Sam Pecker ? He can do it.

(MARCIA BRENT, *the Royds' married daughter, enters* L., *carrying a Japanese basket which she puts on the table.*)

MARCIA. He's busy mopping the salad dressing off the back seat. (*She moves below the table and up* R. *of it.*)

MILDRED (*above the table : dramatically*). The bottle's broken !

MARCIA. No, only oozed a bit. (*Catching sight of a lot of chip baskets fitted into one another on the table.*) What on earth are those for ?

(ARTHUR *rises and exits* L.)

MILDRED (L. *of her*). Brambles, my dear, they ruin the ordinary ones. We must all go blackberrying to-morrow and I want every one of those filled to take back with us. I'll make the jam at home on Monday.

MARCIA. Oh ! Here's a wire I opened. (*She produces a telegram.*) Miranda's arriving at six-fifteen.

MILDRED. Miranda ? But I asked her for *next* week-end.

(ARTHUR *re-enters with a creel.*)

MARCIA. Well, apparently she's coming this.

MILDRED. What's the date, Arthur ? (*Crossing and looking closely at the calendar on the wall* L.) It's—oh, (*clucking exasperatedly*) this must come down, wild geese or no wild geese. It's so misleading. I mean, it's not even last year. (*She crosses* R., *tearing up the calendar and throwing it on the fire.*)

ARTHUR (*sits* L.). It's the twelfth.

MILDRED (*turning at the fireplace*). I swear I never said the twelfth—or did I ? Oh dear, it's most provoking. You see, there is this girl Denys has invited this week-end.

MARCIA (*turning to* MILDRED). Well, there are two beds in the front room. Miranda can sleep with her.

MILDRED. She'll have to. (*Crossing to above the table.*) It *is* annoying, though.

MARCIA. I can't see why. (*Moving down below the settee to the fireplace.*) She can help with the blackberrying, and we've been fuller than this before to-day.

MILDRED. It isn't that, it's—— (*She stops.*)

MARCIA (*to the settee*). What ?

MILDRED. Oh, nothing. I'm just afraid Miranda may be upset about this girl. I mean, he's always talked so much about his work to Miranda and of course she—oh, never mind. We must get on. The beds have to be made up.

ARTHUR. One of you should be thankful that this rod *seems* all right.

MILDRED. See if everything's in from the car, Marcia. Do something to the fire, Arthur. Not that it's cold, but it airs the house.

(BELLA *enters* L. MARCIA *goes out* L., *taking the baskets with her.*)

Did you get the door open ?

BELLA (C.). Yes. Well now, wot about the beds, m'm ? And 'oo's goin' where ?

MILDRED. Mr. and Mrs. Brent in the back room, and Miss . . . what was her name, Arthur ?

ARTHUR. I don't know. I can't keep track of Denys's discoveries.

MILDRED. Dale—I think it's Dale. Miss Dale and Miss Bute in the room next to ours. (*She busies with parcels, and unwraps a ham.*)

BELLA. I didn't know Miss Miranda was comin'.

ARTHUR. Neither did we, but it seems she is.

BELLA (*crossing* L.). I like Miss Miranda. 'Er and me 'as the same taste in films.

(*She exits* L.)

ARTHUR. D'you think the week-end will ever come when we can have the place to ourselves for a change ?

MILDRED. I doubt it. (*Crossing to* ARTHUR *and showing the ham.*) D'you think that bit of ham will do Sunday's breakfast as well as to-night ?

ARTHUR. Depends on people's appetites.

MILDRED. I wish I'd got a whole one. Carve it thinly, Arthur, and spread it about—you know.

ARTHUR. I know.

MILDRED (*returning to the table*). Of course, there's the chicken for to-night, too——

(*Enter* SALLY *at the door* L. *with a bag of tomatoes.*)

SALLY. Hullo !

MILDRED. Hullo, Sally my dear.

SALLY (*crossing to* L. *of the table*). Here are the tomatoes.

MILDRED. My dear, how kind. (*Taking the bag.*) Did your mother send them ?

SALLY. No, Sam made me go for them.

MILDRED. Thank you so much. (*She puts the bag on the table.*)

SALLY. I say, hasn't Miranda Bute got all grown-up. I hardly recognized her.

MILDRED (*looking sharply at* SALLY). Do you mean she is here ?

(ARTHUR *glances up*.)

SALLY. Yes, she's talking to Bella. (*She moves above the table to above the settee.*)

(*Enter* MIRANDA *at the door* L.)

MIRANDA. Aunt Mildred ! (*She crosses to the table.*)
MILDRED. Hello, Miranda dear ! Well, how nice to see you ! (*Kissing her.*)
MIRANDA. It's lovely to see you, and Uncle Arthur. (*She goes to* ARTHUR *and kisses him.*) What an adorable cottage ; I wish we had one like it.
MILDRED. It is nice to come down to. The town is all very well, but a rest in the country at the week-ends makes all the difference. Arthur, get a few sticks for that fire—it's going out. If there aren't any chopped, chop some.
ARTHUR (*rising and making for the garden door*). That'll make a nice rest.

(*He goes out into the garden.*)

MIRANDA (*crossing down* R. *Airily*). Is Denys coming down this week-end ?

(SALLY *is watching* MIRANDA *adoringly.*)

MILDRED. Yes. He and Jim are coming down in his car. They should be here any moment now. Now make yourself at home, dear. I won't be a minute. Keep an eye on the fire, will you ?

(*She goes out.* MIRANDA *kneels by the fire to coax it.* SALLY *sits on the arm of the sofa, feet on the seat.*)

SALLY. You're looking frightfully sort of posh these days.
MIRANDA. Don't be a chump.
SALLY. You are. (*Gloomily reflective, her chin on her hand.*) I wish I wasn't so *sordid*.
MIRANDA. Talk sense.
SALLY. I am. I'm foully healthy, I eat like a horse, my eyelashes won't grow, I don't wonder why I was born, and I *like* school. It couldn't be much more unromantic.
MIRANDA (*rising*). Well, I'm exactly the same. (*She stands with her back to the fire.*)
SALLY. No. You've got a something. (*Suddenly.*) I'd love to be wistful and interesting.
MIRANDA. Oh, Lord !
SALLY. I practised a marvellous expression in the glass but it didn't come off when I tried it out. It's hell having elder brothers.

MIRANDA. It's more hellish not having them.

SALLY. You've always had the Royd boys.

MIRANDA. It's not the same. They're older—and they're not my brothers.

SALLY. That saves you a lot of fun-and-games with ghosts in the night, and always having to play goal.

(MILDRED *re-enters* L., *and hurries up* C. *to the window.*)

MILDRED (*as she goes up*). Where's Sam Pecker ? There's no lettuce that I can find. He is a wretch——

SALLY (*getting off the sofa*). Oh ! Mary Jarrow was here and I heard her say she'd buy some at the shop—yours had gone to seed. (*She moves to above the* R. *end of the table.*)

(MIRANDA *sits on the* L. *arm of the chair above the fire.*)

MILDRED. It seems to me our neighbours do most of Pecker's work for him.

(DENYS *enters with a tent, at the garden door.*)

Oh, you're here at last ! Where's Jim ?

DENYS (*tensely*). Outside. I have never yet murdered a little chee-ild, have I ? (*He comes down* L.C., *below the steps.*)

MILDRED (*coming down a pace*). No, dear. Why ?

DENYS. Well, if I'm left with that proud parent much longer I shall undoubtedly murder my nephew—or his father. (*He flings the tent down.*)

MILDRED. Don't listen. Poor Jim, he can't help it. (*She moves up a step to the window.*)

DENYS (*looking across at* MIRANDA, *in surprise*). Hello !

MIRANDA. Hello.

DENYS. I didn't know you were going to be here. (*He crosses above* SALLY *to above the settee.*)

MILDRED (*coming down* L.C.). It's a pleasant surprise for you.

DENYS. Very—she's the bane of my existence. Aren't you ?

MIRANDA. I didn't know I was.

(MILDRED *crosses to the armchair* L. *and sits.*)

SALLY. What is a " bane " ?

DENYS. A person who has a passion for keeping other people's noses to the grindstone.

SALLY. Oh. Then Mother's more than a bit of a bane.

DENYS. Never mind. (*Indicating* MIRANDA.) I'm making plans to elude her clutches.

MIRANDA (*rising*). P'raps I won't let you.

DENYS. P'raps you won't be able to stop me. (*To* SALLY.) And who are you infuriating at the moment ? (*Tweaking her ear.*)

SALLY. No one. I'm being helpful.

DENYS (*down between the settee and the table*). Then you can't be well.

(ARTHUR *enters from the garden, with a few sticks under his arm and carrying a saucer of water.*)

ARTHUR. They were *not* chopped. The midges are the devil just now. (*He crosses above the settee to the fire.*)

MILDRED. I refuse to sympathize. If you would use some of my stuff——

ARTHUR. No, thank you. (*He places the saucer on the mantel-piece.*) I object to smelling like a ripe Stilton dipped in lavender. (*To* DENYS.) Did you get the tent ?

DENYS. I did. That's it.

(MIRANDA *helps* ARTHUR *at the fire.*)

SALLY. Are you going to sleep in a tent ?

DENYS. I'm going to try to.

SALLY (*moving towards the tent, up* L.C.). I can tell you how to put it up. I was a Girl Guide for a bit once.

MILDRED. Sally, I don't want to appear inhospitable, but you can't stay to supper to-night. There are too many of us already.

SALLY. Of *course* not. (*Above the table.*) I just came over with a message from Mother—only I've forgotten what it was.

ARTHUR (*on his knees*). Then you'd better go back and ask her, hadn't you ?

SALLY. D'you think so ?

MILDRED. I do indeed—it might be important.

(DENYS *moves towards* SALLY.)

SALLY. She wouldn't have sent me if it was. Anyway, I expect I shall remember it in a minute.

DENYS (*taking her by the scruff of the neck*). Off you go. (*As he pushes her up to the garden door :*)

SALLY. I'm sure to remember it the moment I get home and it'll just be a waste of shoe-leather.

(*She is forcibly evicted and disappears.* DENYS *comes down* C., *to the table.*)

MIRANDA (*turning*). Tell me about the Osborne Festival, Denys. I'm longing to hear about it.

(ARTHUR, *rising from the fire, busies himself* R., *examining some casts.*)

DENYS. There's nothing to tell.

MIRANDA (*kneeling on the sofa, facing him*). Didn't you get it after all ?

DENYS. No—at least, I did get the offer of it, but I turned it down.

MIRANDA (*anxiously*). What went wrong ?

DENYS. Nothing, really, but I'm going to Hollywood instead.

(MIRANDA, *stricken, stands, then sits on the settee, facing front.*)

MIRANDA. Hollywood ? (*Pulling herself together.*) Well, I suppose that's an even greater honour—in a way—but—— Is that what you meant by " evading my clutches " ?

DENYS. Perhaps.

MIRANDA. When do you go ?

DENYS. In about four weeks—I think. Nothing's really settled yet.

MIRANDA (*turns away a little. After a short pause*). Whom are you going to work for ? It'll be quite different from stage designing, won't it ? Are you—are you sure you'll like it ?

DENYS. I expect so, because you see I'm not doing designing over there. I decided I was getting stale, so I'm going as Paul Perry's secretary. He's got a contract for two years.

MIRANDA (*turning to face him, appalled*). But . . . You *weren't* getting stale ! That's an absolute whopper—it was exactly the other way round. I don't understand . . .

DENYS. Be a good girl and don't try to.

MILDRED. Denys, dear, you'd better get that tent up. Or at least see that it works, before—well, get it up.

(DENYS *moves up* L.C.)

DENYS (*picking up the tent*). Right.

MIRANDA (*rising*). Can I come ?

DENYS. Not if you're going to argue all the time.

MIRANDA (*to above the settee*). But I don't understand . . .

DENYS. Right—then you stay here.

MIRANDA. All right. I won't talk about it—for the moment.

DENYS (*moving up to the window*). Let me know when Rowena comes. I said seven. They're driving her over from Marton.

MIRANDA (*up* R.C.). Who's Rowena ?

DENYS (*turning to her*). My *very* latest. Wait and see !

MIRANDA. She's coming here ?

DENYS (*turning to the garden door*). She is. Come on.

(*He exits and* MIRANDA *follows him out.*)

MILDRED. Arthur, what are we to do ?

ARTHUR (*turning from the fire but still preoccupied with casts, etc.*). What about ? (*He crosses* C., *with casts and the saucer of water.*)

MILDRED. Oh Arthur, don't be so dull ! About Miranda. It's Denys's fault. She's hero-worshipped him for years and he's encouraged her.

ARTHUR (*at the table*). Rot. He's old enough to be her father and he treats her like a brother.

MILDRED.   I'm very fond of Miranda—and I'm afraid she's going to be hurt.

ARTHUR.   Who's going to hurt her ?   (*He is examining a cast, facing half* R.)

MILDRED.   Denys.   (*She rises and crosses to him.*)   My dear, you can't be so blind that you can't see the child thinks she's in love with him ?

ARTHUR.   Miranda ?   In love ?   Absolute rubbish !   How old is she ?   Fifteen ?

MILDRED.   Seventeen.   That's half the trouble.   Denys still thinks of her as a child—and she isn't a child any more.   She's growing up.   At seventeen, you know, you're very—vulnerable.

(ARTHUR *looks round at her.*)

(*Becoming practical again.*)   I must see about the supper. Watch the fire, there's a good man.

(*She goes out* L.   ARTHUR *returns to the* R. *of the settee with the cast in the saucer.*   SAM PECKER *enters up* L. *from the garden with a bucket of coal.*)

SAM.   Good evenin', sir.   (*He brings the bucket down to the fire.*)

ARTHUR.   Good evening, Pecker.

SAM (*putting a few special pieces on the fire*).   Gettin' every-thin' into trim, I see.

ARTHUR (*rising and putting the saucer on the table across the settee*).   That's the idea.   How's the water ?

SAM.   We could do with a bit of wet.

ARTHUR (*sitting on the settee*).   Some of us were talking about the salmon up here the other night, Pecker ; and of a far from legal form of sport that seems to be rife at the moment.

SAM.   Poaching.   (*Rising.*)   Well, that's true enough, or so I 'ear.

ARTHUR.   This is a good time for it, is it ?

SAM.   We-ell, so they're sayin', sir.   Not, of course, as 'ow I——

ARTHUR.   No, no, of course not.   All the same, I'd like a word with you on the subject later on.

SAM (*slightly apprehensive*).   Yes, sir.   (*He crosses to* C.)

ARTHUR (*turning towards* SAM).   Have you been fishing—in the ordinary way, lately ?

SAM.   I 'aven't been out for a day or so meself, sir, but Billy Spence did none so badly the evenin' befer last.   'Alf a dozen averagin' three-quarters 'e got.

ARTHUR.   Where ?

SAM.   Above the runner by Swale's farm—that stretch.

ARTHUR (*with a quick move*).   Hey, but that's——!

SAM.   Mr. Barasford's, I know, sir.   But you know what Billy is.   And after all, wot the eye doesn't see . . . eh, sir ?   (*He grins.*)

(ADRIAN BARASFORD, *middle-aged, gentle, polite, appears in the garden. He enters and comes down* c.)

ARTHUR. Quite.

SAM (*swinging round and muttering*). Talk of the devil . . .

ARTHUR (*turning on the settee to face* ADRIAN). Good evening, Adrian.

ADRIAN. I heard you arrive and I thought I'd just slip across. Good evening, Pecker.

SAM. 'Evenin', Mr. Barasford, sir. (*Eyeing him uneasily.*) I'll—er—there's some sticks to chop—if you'll excuse——

(*He darts out of the door* L.)

ADRIAN (*shaking hands across the table*). And how are you, Arthur ? (*Looking at* ARTHUR'S *fishing materials which are strewn all over the place.*) Are you thinking of fishing to-night ?

ARTHUR. Thinking, but that's all. I have to entertain our guests to-night. I promised Mildred.

ADRIAN. Pity.

ARTHUR. To-morrow, though. I hear the river's very low.

ADRIAN (*coming below the settee to* R.). Very. Unless it rains to-night I'm afraid it won't be much good. (*He stands facing* ARTHUR.) It's exceedingly vexing. Still, of course, we can try.

ARTHUR. Of course we can.

ADRIAN. Dry fly's the most likely bet, I think. I made myself a very jolly little fellow the other day. I brought him over to show you. (*He produces a small box from his pocket.*)

(MILDRED *enters* L.)

MILDRED. Arthur—good evening, Adrian—Arthur, have you seen the veal-and-ham pie ?

ARTHUR. No, dear.

MILDRED (*going up to the bay*). It was with the brown loaf in the basket with the broken handle. (*Moving out of the garden door.*) Denys !

DENYS (*off*). Hello !

MILDRED		(*At the garden door*). Have you got the basket with the pie and the brown loaf in ?
DENYS		(*Off*). No !
MILDRED		Have you seen it ?
DENYS.	(*overlapping.*)	No!
ARTHUR		What would be the best plan ? Your stream to-morrow and my bit of the river on Sunday ?
ADRIAN		Or vice versa. Whichever you like.

MILDRED (*re-entering*). *Someone* must have had it. I know I put it in. Oh, good heavens, of course! (*Going out again.*) Denys!

DENYS (*off*). Hello!

MILDRED. It's under the back seat in your car. Will you get it out and hand it through the kitchen window? Thank you, dear. (*Coming in again.*) What a relief! How are you, Adrian? (*Crossing down to the door* L.)

ADRIAN. Very well, really, thank you.

MILDRED. I'm so glad.

(*She exits* L.)

ADRIAN (*to* ARTHUR *who is looking at the " spider "*). Rather fine, don't you think? I believe he's a real killer.

ARTHUR. Bit small, isn't he?

ADRIAN. Not at all. Just the right size. Succulent, don't you think? I could almost take him myself.

ARTHUR. Talking of taking things, I've just been asking Pecker about the salmon——

ADRIAN. I told you not to mention the word salmon to me!

ARTHUR. But——

ADRIAN. It makes my blood boil . . . this poaching, I mean. Not that I have any salmon fishing myself, but—— D'you know there was another one poached while I was in town on Wednesday! (*Moving below the settee to* C.)

ARTHUR. Keep calm. I only mentioned it to see if you remembered Wednesday night.

ADRIAN (*turning,* R. *of the table*). Remembered? D'you mean the dinner? Of course I remember. What d'you mean?

ARTHUR. Do you still maintain that poaching salmon is easy —that there's no skill in the business?

ADRIAN (*snorting*). None at all. (*To above the table.*) It's wanton vandalism. Why, a baby in arms could " snatch " a salmon.

ARTHUR. Rather a clever baby, surely. I mean when you've found your salmon you've got to get him first stroke.

ADRIAN. You keep on saying that, Arthur, but what you don't realize is that the poor thing is paralysed, blinded, stupefied by the light from the flares—or very powerful electric torches I believe they use sometimes——

ARTHUR (*rising, to the fireplace*). You seem to know all about it.

ADRIAN. I ought to. I hear enough about it from the Bench.

ARTHUR (*turning to face* ADRIAN). That's why you got so worked up on Wednesday?

ADRIAN. Did I get worked up?

ARTHUR. Then you don't remember so very well?

ADRIAN (*moving to above the settee*). I don't know what you're talking about.

ARTHUR.   You were exceedingly rude to me, Adrian, after the port.

ADRIAN.   I ?   Rude ?   What did I do ?

ARTHUR.   You called me a liar.

ADRIAN (*backing a step*).   Did I ?   What about ?

ARTHUR.   Poaching salmon.   (*To the* R. *edge of the settee.*) You even went so far as to lean across the table, wag your finger under my nose and say : " Arthur, you're a liar—I'll bet you five pounds you're a liar ! "   You then went on to elaborate.

ADRIAN.   I can't believe it.

ARTHUR.   I hardly could at the time.   Nevertheless, I accepted the challenge—in front of witnesses.   You said *anyone* could gaff a salmon first try——

ADRIAN.   And I *still* say so.

ARTHUR.   I said it required skill and no amateur could do it. Didn't I ?

ADRIAN.   You did, Arthur.

ARTHUR.   Right.   Then you made a bet with me.

ADRIAN.   Let's overlook the bet.   The point is——

ARTHUR.   Overlook it ?   I'm damned if I will !   The bet's on —and you're going through with it, me lad !

ADRIAN.   But, Arthur——

(MILDRED *enters* L.   *She is carrying a large vase with water in it, which she puts on the table.*)

MILDRED.   Mary's coming up the road.   Arthur, (*a pause*) something's not quite right upstairs.   I wish you'd have a look at it before the strange guest arrives.   Here's a piece of string— the strongest I could find—I think you'll need it.   See if you can do something—it's so very awkward.   I must try to find a few flowers.   Talk to Mary, Adrian.   I won't be a minute.

(*She goes up into the garden.*)

ARTHUR (*crossing below the settee to* L.C.).   This house is held together with bits of string and safety pins.

ADRIAN (*to above the table* C.).   Did she say Mary was coming ?

ARTHUR (*turning at* L.C.).   Yes.   (*Unknotting the string.*)

ADRIAN.   Mary Jarrow ?

ARTHUR.   I imagine so.   Why ?

ADRIAN.   Oh, nothing.

ARTHUR (*taking the last knot out of the string*).   Don't you like her, or something ?

ADRIAN.   Yes.   (*Almost defiantly.*)   As a matter of fact, I like her very much.

ARTHUR (*faintly surprised at his vehemence*).   Then that's all right.

ADRIAN (*moving towards* ARTHUR).   But it isn't—that's just the trouble.

ARTHUR. What *are* you talking about ?

ADRIAN. I—I—more than like her—I'm—very fond of her.

ARTHUR. So am I. (*Suddenly realizing.*) D'you mean——?
(*He stops.*)

ADRIAN (*abruptly*). Yes. I have for months.

ARTHUR. Good heavens ! I didn't know——

ADRIAN. Nobody knows.

ARTHUR. Not even Mary ?

ADRIAN. Of course not. But I decided this week-end I'd have
to tell someone.

ARTHUR. You'd better consult Mildred. She might be able
to arrange something.

ADRIAN. No, no. A little advice, perhaps, but I don't want
any arrangements——

ARTHUR. You shouldn't need them. Damn it all, you're
here, practically next door to her, all the year round——

ADRIAN. I know, but—— Hush ! Don't say anything.
(*Backing to* R.C.)

(MARY *appears in the doorway* L.)

ARTHUR. Good evening, Mary. Mind the step !

MARY (*entering*). I always do. (*Crossing* ARTHUR.) Hello,
Adrian. I haven't seen you for days. (*At* C.) Arthur dear,
there are your lettuces and you owe me fourpence—or Mildred
does. Where is she ?

ARTHUR. Picking flowers. Forgive me if I get on with a
rather urgent job.

(*He exits* L.)

MARY (*turning to smile at* ADRIAN, *who is thrown into confusion*).
Well, Adrian ! You know, if the Royds didn't come down for
the week-ends, you and I would hardly meet each other from
one month to the next.

ADRIAN (R. *of the settee*). Oh, surely . . . don't you think
. . . ?

MARY. No, I don't. Some day I shall send you a formal
invitation to dinner.

ADRIAN. Do, do. I really wish you would.

(JIM BRENT *enters* L.)

JIM (*calling*). Marcia ! (*He trips down the step.*) Bother that
step !

MARY. Good afternoon, Jim. (*They shake hands.*) Your
wife isn't here.

JIM. Good afternoon. D'you know where she is ?

MARY. I'm afraid I don't.

JIM (*crossing and shaking hands*). How d'you do, sir ? It's
the holiday question, you know.

MARY. What is ?

JIM (*earnestly*). It's so difficult to decide. Of course we've left it rather late. I called at Cook's and got these. (*He puts some holiday pamphlets on the table.*)

ADRIAN. You seem to have brought plenty.

MARY. How's the son-and-heir ?

JIM (*delighted*). Absolutely grand ! By Jove, you know, he grows every day, he really does. It's amazing how they start doing new tricks, too. You're never dull with a child in the house. D'you know the other day when I came downstairs, he was sitting in his pram——

(ARTHUR *enters* L.)

ARTHUR. Jim ! The very person I was looking for ! Go upstairs—d'you know anything about plumbing ?

(MARY *sits on the top arm of the settee.*)

JIM (*crossing*). I think so——

ARTHUR. Here's the string. Go and plumb. I've opened the trap-door for you. You're thinner than I am, it'll be easier for you.

JIM. Well, I don't mind having a try. Upstairs ?

ARTHUR. Upstairs. You can't miss it.

JIM (*with sudden realization*). Oh ! I see.

(*He goes out* L.)

ARTHUR. There's no point in having a handy son-in-law if you don't use him. What about slipping down to the Bridge and having a look at the river ?

ADRIAN. Well—all right. (*To* MARY.) Will you come ?

MARY. No. I'll wait and see Mildred.

(ADRIAN *crosses above her to* R.C.)

ARTHUR. Tell her I won't be five minutes.

(*The door opens and* ELLA SPENDER, SALLY'S *mother, enters, almost bumping into* ARTHUR. *She is untidy and talks almost incessantly and very quickly.*)

ELLA. How d'you do, everyone ? I just walked in. Oh, Adrian, did you find the wretched concert tickets ?

ADRIAN. Yes, yes, they were on the mantelpiece after all.

ELLA (*crossing to* C.). That's all right—as long as you've bought some. You won't bother to use them, will you ? (*Turning to* ARTHUR.) Where's Mildred ?

ARTHUR. In the garden. Call her yourself, Ella, will you ? We're playing truant.

ELLA. Going to the river—I know, only too well. Robert's

exactly the same—perfectly happy as long as he can dangle a piece of string in the water. I'll call her. Off you go.

ARTHUR. Give Robert my kind regards.

ELLA. I will. (*She goes to the window up* c. *and calls :*) Mildred . . . Mildred . . .

MILDRED (*off*). Hullo, Ella my dear.

(ADRIAN *crosses to* ARTHUR *at* L.C. *They exit* L.)

ELLA. Shall I come out ?

MILDRED. No, I'll come in.

(ELLA *comes down* c.)

ELLA (*to* MARY). Oh, I'm distracted about to-morrow night. I suppose you wouldn't like to sing—or give a talk ?

MARY. There is nothing I should like less.

ELLA. I thought so.

(*Enter* MILDRED *from the garden.*)

MILDRED (*coming down* R. *of* ELLA). Oh, the garden is a joy—but there is so much to do.

(MARCIA *enters* L.)

MARCIA. Hello, everybody.

ELLA. Hello !

MILDRED. I wish somebody would stop those wretched children breaking down our fence.

ELLA. D'you mean mine ? They *will* climb——

MILDRED. Of course I didn't mean yours. We must get Jim to mend it.

MARY. Oh, Jim brought these for you, Marcia. (*Indicating the pamphlets.*)

MILDRED. What are they ?

MARCIA, L. *of the table, picks some of them up, glancing through them.*)

ELLA. Holiday Resorts—oh, how exciting ! We used to get these every year and simply pore over every one of them. Of course we went to Filey just the same in the end.

(*The others pick up and examine the pamphlets.*)

MARCIA. " Golf Course of Britain," " Famous Golfing Resort," I thought so.

MARY. Here's Portugal.

ELLA. And Brittany——

MARCIA (*brightening*). That's better.

MILDRED. And " The Golfer Abroad." (*She puts down her pamphlet.*) What are the blackberries like ?

ELLA. Marvellous, but you're just in time.

MILDRED. We must all be out early to-morrow. Sit down, Ella.

ELLA. No, thank you—if I do I'll never get up again. I just popped over to remind you of to-morrow's concert. I expect you'd completely forgotten it.

MILDRED (*lying*). Forgotten ! My dear, we're all agog ! Have we bought our tickets ?

ELLA. Arthur bought a dozen last week.

MARCIA. I didn't know there was going to be a concert. How splendid. (*Moving to the armchair* L.)

ELLA (*to* L.C.). That's the last thing it'll be. It'll be *awful* ! I've arranged them ever since Madge Popham moved and I assure you it'll be simply *frightful*. I must have arranged more frightful concerts than anyone living. Luckily the village is used to me now and they know what to expect.

MILDRED. The hall is always packed. (*She goes up* C. *to the small table by the* R. *pillar*.)

ELLA (*following up towards her*). Yes, but those who don't come out of pure kindness of heart, come out of interest to see if it can possibly be worse than the last. It always is.

MILDRED. Have a cigarette. Oh, there are some here. (*On the little table by the chair*.) Do have one ?

ELLA. No, thank you. I'm calling at the Vicarage and the old lady objects to the smell of smoke. (*She moves towards the garden door*.)

MILDRED. My dear, is there anything she doesn't object to ?

ELLA. I've allowed myself half an hour to hear all about that poor woman's troublesome inside. You know, she just doesn't realize what a crashing bore she is. Oh ! (*Turning at the garden door*.) Have you sent your subscription yet ?

MILDRED. Subscription ? Oh, the organ bellows. No, not yet.

ELLA. Then send it quickly. They're calling in person this week-end on everyone who hasn't sent it. That's why I'm going along with mine.

MILDRED. I'll warn Arthur.

ELLA (*turning to the garden door*). I must go. (*She checks, looking off* L.) Oh, who's the girl with Denys ?

(MARCIA *and* MILDRED *rush to the window*.)

MILDRED (*anxiously*). Girl ? (*Looking out of the window*.) Only Miranda—don't give me such frights !

ELLA (*returning*). Dear me ! She's getting quite good-looking. My family are all so plain, it's *dreadful*.

MILDRED. How are they ? We've seen Sally, of course——

ELLA. Revolting, simply revolting. We've had a terrible week—if they haven't fallen into the river they've fallen into something worse. (*Moving to the garden door*.) Good-bye.

(*Turning back again.*) Oh, good gracious, I've never told you why I came.

MILDRED (*who has come down into the room again*). The concert.

ELLA (*up* L.C.). That wasn't it. Sally told me Miranda was here and I wanted to borrow her. Patience Gover's got laryngitis and she was doing a sketch with Sally. D'you think Miranda would do it instead—or is she too grown up now ?

MILDRED. I don't know. I'll ask her—— (*Moving up towards the window.*)

ELLA. No, don't ask her now, she might say " No," and I couldn't in fairness encourage her to say " Yes." It's a dreadful sketch—I chose it. Look, I'll leave her a copy of it and you try to persuade her. Tell her we're rehearsing in the hall to-morrow afternoon. (*She gives* MILDRED *a copy of the sketch.*)

MARY. D'you want any help with the hall ?

ELLA. No, thank you, we decorated to-day. It's simply hideous, but no one will look at it. I think you're a wretch, though, to refuse to sing, or recite, or something.

(JIM *enters* L.)

MILDRED. If you want talent, here's the very man for you. Jim sings—don't you, Jim ?

JIM (*self-consciously*). Oh well, I don't know—a bit——

ELLA. Do you ? (*Coming down* L.C., *to him.*) But how splendid ! I didn't know. Oh, you *must* come.

JIM. But what is it ?

MARCIA (*by the* L. *pillar*). A concert in the village hall, to-morrow.

JIM. But I haven't any music here.

ELLA. We'll get some for you—or you can hum the tune to Miss Appleyard—she's wonderful at picking things up. This is marvellous, and it'll make such a nice change. What do you sing ?

MARCIA. Only two songs.

ELLA. That'll be heaps. What are they ?

JIM. Couple of things called " Glorious Devon " and " Drake Is Going West, Me Lads."

ELLA. Oh ! (*Crestfallen.*) Oh dear ! That's rather awkward.

MARY. Why ?

ELLA. Well, you see, Tom Mace the water-bailiff always sings those two songs—and you know how difficult it is to break the tradition of years in a place like this.

MILDRED (*coming down the steps and to the flowers on the table*). Can't you sing anything else, Jim ?

MARCIA. No, he can't. It took him years to learn those two.

ELLA. I *am* so sorry, but you see how it is ? And asking

Tom Mace to change would be like suggesting the sun should go backwards—and equally useless. What a pity. Do learn some others for next time. (*She crosses him to the door* L.)

MARCIA. You don't know what you're asking.

ELLA (*at the door*). We do *need* new talent so badly.

MILDRED. Is Robert singing his song ?

ELLA. He is. Honestly I don't know how he *dare*. I *must* fly. (*She opens the door.*)

MILDRED. Mind the step.

ELLA. Oh yes, of course. Good-bye.

(*She exits, closing the door.*)

JIM (*to* L. *of the table* C.). Funny that Tom Mace sings those same songs. Well—well—well—— (*Turning up to face* MARCIA.) What about a stroll, Marcia darling ?

MARCIA. There's a lot to do——

MILDRED. Nonsense ! You're here as guests—more or less. Away you go. Supper's at half-past seven—I hope.

MARCIA. We'll only squabble about holidays.

MILDRED. Then I'd much prefer you to squabble outside. Go on.

MARCIA. All right. (*Going down* L., *followed by* JIM.) Where shall we go ? Mind the step.

JIM. What about over the golf course ?

MARCIA (*as she disappears,* JIM *following*). *No !*

MILDRED. Considering the way they persistently quarrel, it's amazing how happy those two are. (*Looking at the flowers she has been arranging in the vase.*) D'you think those look better or worse than nothing ?

MARY. Better. Very pretty. My dear, (*rising*) I must go.

MILDRED. I wish I could ask you to supper, but we're so many and Sally's sure to come back on some pretext or another just as we're starting, so——

MARY. I shouldn't dream of staying.

MILDRED (*crossing down below the settee to* R.). Come to tea on Sunday, when we all know our guest better.

MARY (*moving up the steps*). And help to eat up the scraps ? I'd love to. Shall I call for you to-morrow night ?

MILDRED. Do.

(MARY *exits into the garden.*)

Oh dear, that fire ! (*She kneels down beside it.*)

(SAM PECKER *comes past the windows,* R. *to* L. *singing. A pause.* MILDRED *puts up the paper in front of the fire and starts to read it at the same time. She is completely absorbed when a voice off* L. *calls :*)

ROWENA (*off*). Hello, there !

MILDRED (*abstractedly*). Hello !

ROWENA. Can I come in ?

MILDRED. Of course. (*Blowing under the paper. A pause. Calling.*) I'm in the sitting-room.

(*The door* L. *opens and* ROWENA MARRIOTT, *tall, lovely, in long trousers and a handkerchief round her head, stands in the doorway.*)

You can come in, but you can *not* stay to supper.

ROWENA. Oh ! Then where can I have it ?

MILDRED. At home—— (*It suddenly dawns on her that that is not* SALLY SPENDER'S *voice, and she turns quickly.*) Oh ! Oh dear ! I'm *so* sorry ! (*Flustered.*) I thought you were someone else. How stupid of me—of course, you're not a bit like her. Do come in—mind the step—down.

ROWENA (*to* L.C.). Oh, thank you. I thought perhaps I'd come to the wrong place. I couldn't find the bell.

MILDRED. No—it is difficult—it's rather round the corner, everyone just walks in. (*Rising and moving to* C., *above the table.*) You're Miss Dale, of course ?

ROWENA. Well, actually my name's Marriott. I say, d'you think I *have* come to the wrong place ?

MILDRED. Oh, perhaps you have——

ROWENA. I'm going to stay with some people called Royd.

MILDRED. Oh, that's quite right. Forgive me for being so stupid. My dear, we're so pleased to see you. Denys has talked such a lot about you.

ROWENA. I hope it *was* me. Perhaps he meant to ask someone else. Is he here ?

MILDRED. Yes. Just one minute. I'll call him. (*She goes up the first step to the windows.*) Of course he meant you—I always get names wrong. This wretched fire won't burn.

ROWENA (*cheerfully*). It's a comic little place this, isn't it ?

MILDRED (*on the steps*). I suppose it is, rather. I must apologize for the untidiness—we have to bring so much with us—and we've just arrived——

ROWENA. I rather like untidiness. I hate houses where you feel you ought to eat your cigarette ends.

MILDRED. Yes—of course——

ROWENA. D'you mind if I go and dismiss my chariot ? I kept him till I was sure it was the right place. (*She moves to the door.*)

MILDRED. Do. I'll call Denys. Mind the step.

(ROWENA *goes out* L.)

(*At the window.*) Denys ! DENYS !

DENYS (*off*). Hello !

MILDRED (*beckoning*). Come here—quickly—your guest!
DENYS (*off*). Coming!
MILDRED. Leave that and come *now*!

(*She bustles back into the room and picks up a paper and a basket.
DENYS enters with MIRANDA.*)

DENYS (*down to* C.). Where is she?
MILDRED. Sending the car away. Didn't you hear it? You should have been listening—she couldn't find the bell and there was no one to welcome her. Why didn't you say what she was like? I'd have planned things differently. We must make arrangements about washing in the morning. I don't think she's been used to our smash-and-grab methods with a bathroom. Go out and help—she'll have a bag.
DENYS. I ought to wash my hands.
MILDRED. You can do that later. Now don't just leave her to me. (*Frowning.*) Go along. Where are your manners?
DENYS (*moving to the door*). Believe me, Rowena won't mind.
MILDRED. Well, *I* do.

(DENYS *goes out* L.)

MIRANDA (*coming down* L.C., *and then to below the settee*). What's she like?
MILDRED (*tidying up*). Very lovely—at least I think so. (*To the dresser* L., *bus.*) I was too upset by her clothes to notice her face much.
MIRANDA (*standing on the hearthrug, her back to the fire*). Are they marvellous?
MILDRED (*crossing to the table*). Trousers, my dear, and one of those brilliant scarves round her head. The magazines can say what they like, but that is *not* the approved wear for the country. Not in Throppleton, anyway. I daren't think what people will say—sh!

(DENYS *and* ROWENA *enter* L.)

ROWENA (*entering*). . . . and the roads in America are marvellous.
MILDRED (*crossing to them*). Now then, come along in and just make yourself at home. We're very informal here, you'll find. (*Returning to the table.*) Oh, let me introduce my niece—Miranda Bute—Miss—Marriott.
MIRANDA. How d'you do?
ROWENA (*to* R. *of* DENYS). How are you? (*Turning to* DENYS.) Is this the one that bosses you about?
DENYS (L.C.). That's the one. She mayn't look much, but when she starts talking there's no stopping her.

(MILDRED *moves up stage, tidying bus. etc.*)

Rowena. I've heard a lot about what she's said. I thought you said she was a child ?

Denys. She's not much more. Two penn'orth of copper— and a ha'penny on the top.

Miranda (*who has not moved from the hearth*). I mayn't be frightfully tall, but I possess ears and my brain works, so you might stop talking about me as though I wasn't here.

Rowena (*to* Denys). Now we've infuriated her. (*She crosses to above the settee.*)

Denys. God forbid ! She's a tigress when roused. (*Crossing below the settee to* R.) Aren't you, my sweet ?

Miranda. Yes—darling pet !

(Denys *sits in the armchair below the fire.*)

Mildred. Would you like to come up to your room ?

Rowena. Not yet—if you don't mind. (*She sits on the settee.*) D'you dress for dinner ?

Denys. Good heavens, no !

Mildred (*down to above the table*). We can't, because we don't have it—only supper, I'm afraid. Two courses ; something, and cheese and biscuits.

Rowena. How sensible. It saves a lot of bother and I'm all for that. (*Stretching on the settee.*) Oh !—the country air makes me feel deliciously lazy.

Denys. Don't blame the country. I've never known you when you felt otherwise.

Rowena. Wait till you see me in America ! (*Lazily.*) All bounce and dash. Honestly, the air there has the most amazing effect on you—on every one.

Miranda. Oh, you're going to America, too, are you ?

Rowena. D'you object ? No, don't answer that—it's unfair. As a matter of fact, it was through me that Paul persuaded Denys to go with him. Paul said he wouldn't and I said he would if he was pressed.

Miranda. And who did the pressing ?

Mildred (*who has listened to this, somewhat disturbed*). Miranda, what about unpacking before Miss—Marriott goes up ? The room's very small—oh, I hadn't broken it to you—I'm afraid you two will have to share a bedroom——

Rowena (*to* Miranda). D'you snore ?

Miranda. No, but it doesn't worry me a bit.

Rowena. That's a blessing. We must have a girlish heart-to-heart after the lights are out, don't you think ?

Miranda. Heavenly.

Rowena. All about Denys and his career.

Miranda. That would have been easier—when he had one.

Denys. What d'you mean ?

Miranda. I thought you'd given it up to go to America ?

DENYS. Did you ?——

ROWENA (*sitting up*). My dear child, d'you know what Perry's paying him to go with him ?

MIRANDA (*furiously*). No—and I don't want to. (*She turns away to the fireplace.*)

ROWENA (*lying back*). That saves me the trouble of remembering what it was.

DENYS (*rising and pulling* ROWENA *up*). Stop sparring with the child and go and unpack. And put a dress on. Mother disapproves of trousers.

MILDRED. Denys ! I never said such a thing—to you—or to—— Don't listen to him, wear just what you like.

ROWENA (*crossing down and over to* L.C.). Oh, I've got a dress, and I was going to put it on, anyway. (*Turning to them* L.C.) Personally, I quite agree in most cases about trousers. Actually, I'm not bad behind. (*Turning to show them.*) You want good mirrors when you buy trousers—and you should make " Behind First " your motto.

MILDRED. Yes—I'm sure—I think—(*as* DENYS *laughs*) Denys, you are ridiculous !

ROWENA (*up* L.C.). Would I throw every one into a frenzy if I had a bath ?

(*By* MILDRED'S *face it becomes obvious she would.*)

DENYS. I expect so. (*Crossing to the armchair* L.) A bath here's an event—and an adventure.

MILDRED. What nonsense ! No, of course you wouldn't. I'll tell Bella to stoke up the fire. Denys, make sure there are towels in Rowena's room. Bella's been rather busy. If not, you know where they are. In the boot-cupboard on the shelf below the jam.

(*She bustles out* L. MIRANDA *sits on the arm of the armchair above the fireplace.*)

ROWENA (*up* C.). So this is Throppleton. What d'you do here, if it's not a rude answer ?

DENYS. Nothing much. Go for walks—and generally laze— weather permitting.

ROWENA. I'm all for lazing, but I rather like it organized.

DENYS. Come on. I'll take your bag up.

(*They move* L.)

ROWENA. I'll try anything once—even the Simple Life.

(ARTHUR *and* ADRIAN *enter from the garden and cross down* R.C. *below the steps.*)

DENYS (*turning at* L.). Hello ! My father, Rowena.

ARTHUR. How d'you do ? (*A little startled by* ROWENA'S *appearance.*)

ROWENA. Frightfully well, thank you.

DENYS. And Mr. Barasford—Rowena Marriott.

ROWENA. How are you ?

ADRIAN. I'm very well, thank you.

ROWENA (*to* ARTHUR). Don't worry, I'm just going to change them.

ARTHUR. Change them ?

ROWENA (*tweaking her trouser-leg*). These. See you later. (*She goes out* L. *with* DENYS. ADRIAN *to the fireplace.*)

ARTHUR. I say ! (*To* L. *of the table* C.) Isn't Denys becoming rather dashing in his old age ?

MIRANDA (*rising*). I think he's becoming idiotic. (*Crossing up to the garden-door.*) I suppose I'll have to finish the tent by myself.

(*She goes out into the garden.*)

ARTHUR (*crossing to above the settee*). To get back to what we were talking about——

ADRIAN. No, no, Arthur—it's impossible.

ARTHUR. On the contrary, I believe it's most possible—if I know my Sam Pecker correctly.

ADRIAN. But——

ARTHUR. Either that or you eat your words and give me a written apology.

ADRIAN. I shall do no such thing. It's the truth——

ARTHUR (*sitting on the top arm of the settee*). Right, then the deal's on.

ADRIAN. But, Arthur, think of my position——

ARTHUR. Think of it yourself. You made a bet—you called me a liar——

ADRIAN. I know, and I'm sorry——

ARTHUR. That's better——

ADRIAN. You were one, of course, but I'm sorry I said so——

ARTHUR. That settles it. (*He rises.*) Because of my kind heart and this position of yours you keep harping on, I'll still agree to do the job, but you'll come along to see fair play.

(*Enter* BELLA *at the door* L.)

BELLA. Excuse me, sir, but the missus says, " How's the fire going ? "

ARTHUR. It isn't, I'm afraid.

BELLA. Half a minnit, I'll fix it.

(*She exits through the door* L.)

ADRIAN. Arthur, think seriously about to-night.

ARTHUR. I shall, and I'll have everything cut and dried by to-morrow.

ADRIAN. No, no, I meant think seriously of it and you'll think better of it.

(*Enter* ROWENA, MILDRED *and* DENYS *by the door* L.)

ROWENA (*to up* L.C.). A slight hiatus.

DENYS (*at the armchair* L.). Whilst the water heats.

MILDRED (*crossing to the table*). I'm so sorry . . . it won't be long now.

ROWENA. Not at all. I enjoy procrastinating. (*She moves up to the garden door.*) Couldn't I be shown round the garden whilst I wait ?

ARTHUR (*moving up* R.C.). I'm afraid it's not that sort of garden.

ROWENA. Oh ! (*Looking at it.*) Perhaps not. Well, come along, Denys dear, lead me into the wilderness.

(ROWENA *and* DENYS *exit at the garden door.*)

ADRIAN (*crossing up* C.). Well, good night. (*He turns to* ARTHUR.) See you to-morrow.

ARTHUR. You most certainly will. Good night.

(*Exit* ADRIAN *into the garden.*)

MILDRED. The water is just faintly tepid. Really, people shouldn't want to wash so thoroughly the moment they arrive in a strange place. (*To the dresser* L.) Now, clear up your things, Arthur, and you'll just have time to do a little weeding before supper.

ARTHUR (*down to above the table*). Look here, what was the idea of having this damned cottage ?

MILDRED (*bus. at the dresser*). I don't know what you mean. To get away from the town, of course.

ARTHUR. And what was the idea of that ?——

MILDRED (*returning to* L. *of the table*). What are you talking about ?

ARTHUR. Well, go on, tell me.

MILDRED. To get into the fresh air and because you know a week-end in the country does you a world of good.

(ARTHUR *gives a peculiar* " Ho ! ho ! ")

What's that ?

ARTHUR. Hollow laughter.

(*Enter* BELLA L., *with an oil can.*)

BELLA (*crossing below the table to* R.). A drop of this should cheer it up.

MILDRED. What is it ?

BELLA. Paraffin.

MILDRED (*moving up* C.). Do be careful.

(MIRANDA *enters through the garden door with a basket of potatoes.*)

MIRANDA. Mr. Pecker says these are all the potatoes there are.
MILDRED. That's not nearly enough.
BELLA (*at the fire*). Here goes ! (*She throws the oil on the fire.*)

(*There is an explosion and soot, bricks, etc., fall.*)

(*As the row and dust die down.*) Well, that's better out than in, as my old mother used to say.

MILDRED. Good gracious ! Look at the mess. I was right, Arthur. We are in for a very difficult week-end. (*As the* CURTAIN *falls, she is saying :* " Get a brush, Bella—quickly. No, better call Sam Pecker . . ." *etc.*)

CURTAIN.

ACT II

Scene 1

Scene.—*The same as Act I. Saturday afternoon.*

As the Curtain *rises* Arthur *is sitting by the table, playing with flies, etc. At the top end of the settee* Marcia *is looking at leaflets of holiday resorts.* Jim, *beside the chair down* L., *is practising chips with a mashie.* Mildred, *standing above the fire, is going steadily through an old cookery book, searching for a special Bramble Jelly recipe.*

Mildred. It's so annoying because I *know* it's here somewhere. Dear me! We haven't had Mock Duck for ages.

Arthur. We had Mock Chicken last night. That was a very old hen, badly disguised.

Mildred. Nonsense! The knife was blunt.

Marcia. Then so were our teeth. Jim, what about Estoril? (*Reading.*) " Sunny plage, bathing, tennis, walks."

Jim. Any golf?

Marcia. I'm afraid so.

Mildred. If the worst comes to the worst, I shall put a pound to a pound and a pint of water and hope for the best.

Marcia. That's too much water for *bramble* jam, surely?

Mildred (*worriedly*). I don't think so. Oh! Here's Aunt Martha's Kidney Pudding.

Arthur. Poor Aunt Martha.

Jim. I wonder if that book of Cotton's would put me right if I got it?

Marcia. I shouldn't think so.

Jim (*swinging the mashie—suddenly*). I believe I know what's wrong. I'm putting my right hand too far over.

Marcia. Then don't put it so far. What about Brittany? It's very cheap.

Jim. Or there's St. Andrews.

(Marcia *looks at him.*)

Marcia. This is supposed to be a holiday for both of us.

Jim. There's some lovely country round Gleneagles.

Mildred. Lovely!

Marcia. Yes, but you'll play golf all day, and what do I do? Walk round the lovely country by myself?

Jim. You could walk round the course with me.

Marcia. Thank you.

Jim. But I wouldn't play all day—only occasionally.

31

MARCIA. Then what's the point in going there ? It's very expensive and that's what you pay for.

JIM. There is that, of course.

(DENYS *and* ROWENA *enter, very wet about the feet, through the garden door.*)

MILDRED. Hello, dear ! Had a nice walk ?

DENYS (*by the* L. *pillar. Blankly.*) Simply heavenly !

ROWENA (*coming to between the table and the settee*). We came back over the downs and everything's dripping.

MILDRED. Your shoes are soaking ! Sit down and take them off—Denys, you should have kept to the roads.

ROWENA. Don't worry, it's quite all right.

MILDRED. It's such disappointing weather. We've picked brambles all the afternoon and they're soaking too. I'd have liked to get them on to-night—but I can't find the recipe and now there isn't time.

ROWENA (*picking up a leaflet from the settee*). Who's going to Majorca ? (*To* MARCIA.) You ?

MARCIA. I wish I was.

JIM (*suddenly*). I've got it ! I'm taking too upright a swing. By Jove, I believe I really have got it this time. Look, sir. (*To* ARTHUR.) Would you mind watching ? Now this is what I *was* doing. (*He swings.*)

MILDRED. Mind my rug ! (*She moves to above the settee, first putting the recipe book on the armchair.*)

MARCIA. Do shut up, Jim. You can practise in the garden later. We *must* settle this holiday question.

ROWENA (*moving* L. *below the table, and up* L.C.). Why not Majorca ? You'd like it. I was there in May.

MARCIA. You see the trouble is Jim wants exercise and I want a rest.

ROWENA. I suppose that does make it difficult.

ARTHUR. Why not a cycling tour through Sweden ?

JIM. A *cycling* tour ?

MILDRED (*to the* R. *end of the table*). That should give you all the exercise you want.

MARCIA. And what about the rest for me ?

DENYS. All right if you buy a tandem and sit behind.

MARCIA. But seriously, it is ridiculous that we can't find somewhere we'd both like.

JIM (*crossing down to* R., *by the fireplace*). Well, you can't beat Scotland, I always say.

DENYS. That must become tedious in time.

JIM. I'll go anywhere you like. I'm fond of golf, but if you're not, I can—and will—do without it.

ROWENA (*dropping down* L.C.). What's the matter with golf ?

MARCIA (*rising angrily and swinging round above the settee*). I *hate* Golfing Resorts ! Besides, golf is absolutely fatal to conversation. Look at Jim.

JIM. What am I doing wrong now ? (*Swinging his club.*)

MARCIA. Nothing——

MILDRED. Except ruining my carpet. Be careful, Jim, please.

MARCIA. It isn't that I mind so much sitting all day while Jim plays, but I do object to sitting all night listening to how he foozled a three-foot putt, or just lipped the bunker (*swinging her arms in demonstration*), or pulled his number four into the rough, or put his second on the edge of the green, or hit the fence at the eighth, or carried the stream at the ninth, or hit a smacking drive but pushed out a bit at the eleventh—— (*She pauses for breath.*)

MILDRED (*catching hold of one wildly swinging arm*). Marcia, dear !

DENYS. It's all right. We're getting rapidly round the course.

MARCIA. I know the thing by heart ! And I do object to having to put up with it when I'm on holiday.

JIM. But I only wish I *could* push my drives out a bit at the moment. My trouble is I'm pulling the damned things.

MARCIA (*viciously*). I shall use weed-killer when it comes to the point.

MILDRED. I think you'd better change the subject and discuss the holiday question later.

MARCIA. Jim can go to Gleneagles, or any other golf course he likes, and I'll stay at home. That *would* be a holiday. (*She sits on the settee.*)

(DENYS *strolls to* R. *and picks up the recipe book.*)

MILDRED. Hush, Marcia, now you're being silly. (*Crossing to* ROWENA.) Give me your shoes, Rowena, and go and change your stockings, dear. (*Taking* ROWENA'S *shoes.*) And you, Denys.

DENYS (*looking through the book*). In a minute.

MILDRED (*crossing* ROWENA, *to the door* L.). And if you come across the recipe for bramble jelly mark it with a piece of paper for me, will you ? (*Turning at the door.*) Marcia, if you and Jim are supposed to be seeing the Waltons before the concert, you'd better be going. Now don't be late—we're too well known.

(*She goes out with the shoes* L. JIM *is swinging his club in front of the fireplace.*)

MARCIA (*rising*). I'll get my things on. Jim, for heaven's sake, give that thing to me.

JIM. Sorry, darling.

(*She snatches his mashie from him.*)

B

MARCIA (*crossing* L.). I wonder how many women curse the day golf was invented.

(*She goes out by the* L. *door.*)

JIM (*crossing below the table to* ROWENA). Marcia doesn't care much for golf.

ROWENA (*seated on the arm of the armchair* L.). I'd almost gathered that.

JIM. Never mind, we've got another golfer in the family. My small son. You must meet him some day. I had a little mashie and putter made for him, and by Jove, he's got quite a good swing already.

ROWENA. How old is he ?

JIM. Just three.

DENYS. Don't encourage him, for God's sake !

JIM (*with elaborate indifference*). I've got some photographs, I believe. . . . (*Fishing in his pocket.*)

DENYS (*moving down* R. *of the settee*). Believe my foot ! You know you have. We had to go miles out of our way yesterday to collect them. (*He turns over some pages of the book.*)

JIM. Perhaps photographs bore you ?

ROWENA (*politely*). Not at all.

JIM (*handing* ROWENA *a snapshot*). Well, there he is with the dog.

DENYS (*without looking up from the book*). The dog's on the left. (*He sits on the arm of the chair above the fire.*)

JIM (*handing another*). I'm afraid he's moved a bit in this one.

ARTHUR. If you really want to know what the child looks like, there's a perfectly good photograph of him on the mantelpiece.

JIM. I always think snapshots are better than set photographs myself.

ROWENA (*examining a snapshot*). I don't think I quite understand this one.

JIM (*over his shoulder*). Which one is that ? Oh ! No, that's not too good. I was a bit late—he had just gone round the corner. That's his foot. He's a comic little fellow, you know. The other day I spilt a drop of beer on the cloth and what do you think he said ?

ROWENA. I don't know.

JIM. Pah ! Dirty boy.

ROWENA. No !

JIM. He did.

DENYS. Don't split your sides. There's worse to come.

(MARCIA *re-enters* L.)

MARCIA. Oh heavens, is he telling you about Richard ? (*Crossing to* L. *of the table.*) Don't believe a word of it. He's quite a nice child, really.

JIM. I never said he wasn't. I may laugh at him sometimes, but——

MARCIA. Forgive him. He can't help it. He's never had a son before.

ROWENA. I'm enjoying myself. (*She smiles sweetly at* JIM.)

MARCIA. Have you got the tickets ?

JIM. What tickets ? Oh, the concert. Yes. Your mother gave them to me.

MARCIA. Then we'd better go.

(ROWENA *hands the photographs back to* JIM *with another ravishing smile.* JIM *is slightly overcome.*)

(*Moving to the door* L.) And I warn you, you mention golf or Richard at the Waltons' only on pain of death.

(*She exits.* JIM *follows to the door.*)

DENYS. Oh, let the poor fellow speak occasionally.

ARTHUR (*rising*). Take no notice of them, Jim. (*He moves round to sit* R. *of the table.*)

JIM (*at the door*). I never do.

DENYS. Mind the step.

(JIM *trips over the step and exits* L.)

ROWENA (*stretching*). I suppose I'd better go and change. Did Perry say when he meant to sail ? (*She strolls across to* R.C., *above the table.*)

DENYS (*rising and moving down* R. *of the settee*). Early next month.

ROWENA. I wish you could come on the same boat with us. We'd have such fun. Oh, did I tell you I'd had a letter from Yvonne Schulter yesterday ? They give the most extraordinary parties.

DENYS. Oh !

ROWENA. We'll go and stay with them, they've got a house right on Malibu beach. They'd love to have you.

DENYS. Don't forget I shall have a certain amount of work to do.

ROWENA. Of course you won't. Authors aren't allowed to work in Hollywood. That's traditional. And if Perry isn't working, you can't.

DENYS. I haven't said definitely that I'm going yet.

ROWENA (*leaning across the settee*). But you are. Aren't you ?

DENYS. Now don't be " arch " with me—and don't pose.

ROWENA. I wasn't consciously doing either.

DENYS. Liar !

(ROWENA *laughs.*)

What was it Mother wanted ? (*Flicking over the pages of the recipe book.*) Ah, " Granny's Sticky Gingerbread." " Hannah's Tea Buns." " Cousin Bob's Rich Lunch Cake——" this is a sort of family album. Ah-ha ! Here we are. " Extra Special Bramble Jam Aunt Florence." (*He sticks a piece of paper in the place, and puts the book down.*)

(MIRANDA *enters from the garden in a macintosh and Wellington boots, carrying a basket.*)

ROWENA (*turning*). Hello ! And where has little Miranda been ?

(MIRANDA *comes down to* L. *of the table.*)

MIRANDA (*in an affected voice*). Just dispensing a few gifts to the poo-er. What did you think ?
DENYS. Don't be a fathead. (*He hunts for his slippers.*)
MIRANDA. Actually I've been rehearsing a *screamingly* funny sketch with Sally Spender and collecting brambles. (*Suddenly and childishly eager.*) Look ! I must have got about three pounds.
ROWENA (*to* C., *above the table*). You're a funny mixture, aren't you ?
MIRANDA. Oh, very. Half faun, half Girl Guide—that's me.
DENYS (*searching by the fire*). Where the hell are my slippers ?
MIRANDA. In the kitchen—I'll get them——
ROWENA. Our little ray of sunlight !
DENYS (*crossing below the table to* L.). Thanks, I'll get them myself.
MIRANDA. Bring mine too, please. (*She goes* R. *below the table to the fireplace and puts down the basket on the chair below.*)

(DENYS *opens the door, meeting* ADRIAN *in the doorway.*)

DENYS. Hello ! Mind the step !
ADRIAN (*entering*). Thank you. Good afternoon.

(*Exit* DENYS.)

ARTHUR. Come in, Adrian. D'you know Miss Marriott ?
ADRIAN (L. *of the table*). We met yesterday. How d'you do ?
ROWENA. Frightfully well, thank you, how are you ?
ADRIAN. I'm very well, thank you. And how are you, Miranda ?
MIRANDA (*imitating* ROWENA's *drawl*). I'm frightfully well, thank you.

(ROWENA *looks at her.*)

ADRIAN. Pity it's been such an unpleasant day, isn't it ? (*To* ROWENA.) You're not seeing our country at its best.

(MIRANDA *sits above the fire ;* ROWENA *is looking at some of* ARTHUR'S *fishing tackle.*)

Hello ! I say ! That's a nice little fellow, Arthur. I've brought some of my own. . . .

(*He sits above the table by* ARTHUR *and takes a fly book out of his haversack. From here onward* ADRIAN *and* ARTHUR *remain engrossed in flies, tackle and fishing ; taking no notice of what is going on around them.* MILDRED *enters* L.)

MILDRED. I hope you have some other shoes, Rowena. (*At* L. *of the table.*) Those won't be dry before morning—if then.

ROWENA. Yes, thanks. I'm just going to change. (*Crossing* MILDRED *to* L. *She yawns.*) Oh, Denys found your bramble recipe.

(*She exits* L.)

MILDRED (*crossing above the table to* R.). Oh, thank you, thank goodness. (*She looks behind* MIRANDA *for it and finds it on the mantelpiece.*) Arthur, Bella says the Vicar called again just before lunch for the organ fund money. Apparently he wants his automatic bellows badly.

ARTHUR. Lot of nonsense. Sam blows very nicely if somewhat erratically, and it relieves the monotony if you don't know whether the next bar's coming or not.

MILDRED. Well, anyway, we promised to subscribe, so take it round or they will call again when we're in.

ARTHUR. Oh Lord, was his mother with him ?

MILDRED. She was.

ARTHUR. I'll go round first thing in the morning.

MILDRED. Why not to-night ?

ARTHUR. I've got a cast to make up.

MILDRED. Very well, but don't blame me if you're caught.

ADRIAN (*startled*). Caught ?

MILDRED. By the Vicar.

ADRIAN. Oh ! Oh, yes, yes, of course.

MIRANDA (*rising*). What did you think she meant ? (*She moves to* R. *of the settee.*)

ADRIAN. Nothing—I just wasn't thinking. . . .

ARTHUR (*kicking him under the table*). Then think, you silly ass.

MIRANDA. I got a lot of brambles. (*Indicating the basket.*) Look ! (*She sits on the settee.*)

MILDRED (*examining the brambles*). Well done ! Oh dear, I wish they'd been drier. (*She puts the basket down by the upper armchair.*) Are *your* feet wet ?

MIRANDA. Not in these. (*Tugging off her Wellington boots.*) Aunt Mildred.

MILDRED (*reading the recipe, from the armchair up* R.). Yes.

MIRANDA. D'you think Denys really will go to America ?

MILDRED. I'm afraid it looks like it.

MIRANDA. You don't want him to, do you ?

MILDRED. No. Naturally I don't. But if it's what he wants to do, I wouldn't try to stop him.

MIRANDA. I would.

(MILDRED *goes to help* MIRANDA *with her Wellingtons.*)

ARTHUR (*to* ADRIAN, *showing him a cast*). That's the cast I used last Saturday.

ADRIAN (*examining it*). Ah !

(MIRANDA *takes the Wellingtons to below the fireplace and puts them down.*)

MILDRED (L. *of her*). My dear, it's no good. If you try to persuade people against their will, you only get the blame afterwards if the thing you persuaded them to do goes wrong.

MIRANDA. But it wouldn't go wrong ! I don't believe he really wants to go. He *can't* ! It's that Rowena woman——

MILDRED (*watching her*). If he's fond of Rowena of course he'll want to go to be near her. Anyway, it's something he must decide for himself, and I wouldn't interfere if I were you.

MIRANDA. But he's talked to me so much about his designing. He told me (*turning away*)—oh, it doesn't matter. I'm being a fool.

MILDRED. I think perhaps you are, rather.

ADRIAN. Good heavens ! The moths have been at this fellow.

MILDRED (*picking up the basket*). You can't control people's lives for them.

MIRANDA. You can tell them what you think. (*She sits in the chair above the fire.*)

MILDRED (*turning up* C.). You can, but you won't—always—if you're sensible.

(DENYS *re-enters* L., *and moves up into the window bay.*)

This rain is most unfortunate. (*Crossing to* L.C.) I'm afraid it's very dull for Rowena. I don't know what we can do. (*Turning at* L.C.) Still, you've had a walk, and of course there's the concert to-night, if she'd like that. (*She moves up* L.C. *towards* DENYS.)

DENYS. We don't want her to have a heart attack from too much excitement.

ADRIAN. That's a Split Butcher. I was getting them all on a Split Butcher on the bob.

DENYS (*by the window*). It's stopped raining and I believe it's going to be a fine night.

MILDRED.   Denys, you're not still insisting on sleeping out ?
DENYS.   Of course I am.
MILDRED.   You're a lunatic—and I take no responsibility.
If you get pneumonia you must nurse yourself.   (*Turning
down* L.)   I must take this to Bella.   Arthur, you'll have to take
all those things off the table in a minute.   I want the supper set
before we go.

(*She goes out* L. *with the basket.*)

MIRANDA.   I'll come and nurse you.
DENYS.   Nobody's going to nurse me.   (*Crossing down above
the settee.*)
ARTHUR.   Have a look at these.   An old client sent them to
me, I can't recognize any of them.   Perhaps he tied them himself.
ADRIAN.   It's an art, tying flies.   An art that is rapidly
dying out, I'm sorry to say.   Where's my book . . . now let me
see. . . .
MIRANDA.   Denys, I want to talk to you.
DENYS (*grimly*).   And I want to talk to you.
MIRANDA.   What about ?   The Osborne job ?   Because——
DENYS.   No.   (*He crosses down to the chair above* MIRANDA.)
ADRIAN.   Oh, a grouse and teal, or very like it.
DENYS (*twisting her hair so that she is unable to move her head*).
Are you going to be civil to Rowena, or are you not ?
MIRANDA.   I've never been uncivil to her.   I've been careful
not to be.
DENYS.   You've got as near it as you damn well dare.
ADRIAN.   You can't beat a Silver Teal, a March Brown and a
Butcher on the bob.
MIRANDA.   I have a perfect right to dislike people if I want to
—just as you have a right to like them—if you want to.
DENYS.   Rowena is a guest here and you're going to be polite.
Understand ?   Not that she cares, but *I* do.
MIRANDA.   The family honour is at stake !
DENYS.   Something like that.   (*He crosses down to the fire
and turns.*)   Anyway, remember what I said or I'll deal with you
as I often have in the past.
MIRANDA.   You're a nice one to be talking about honour—
family or any kind.   I suppose you've forgotten you used to talk
to me about artistic integrity once.
DENYS.   I swear I never used such an expression.
MIRANDA.   You did.
DENYS.   I must have been very young.
MIRANDA.   It wasn't so very long ago.
DENYS.   Well, I have forgotten—and I hope you'll forget it,
too.   (*He sits on the settee.*)
MIRANDA.   I won't.
ADRIAN.   When I was at Loch Leven——

ARTHUR. Just a minute.

MIRANDA. Denys, if you go away it'll take you years to get back to where you are now.

DENYS. In America with Perry I shall have an income four times the size I could hope to earn here—for years, anyway. That weighs more than a little with me, believe me.

ARTHUR. That's a Whimbrel. Got it from an American up at Lairg.

ADRIAN. " Whimbrel " means " curlew," I believe.

MIRANDA. You'll get out there and start regretting it the moment you do. I'm sure of that.

DENYS. Then I can come home.

MIRANDA. But you'll have missed the Osborne job.

DENYS. I could get it another year.

MIRANDA. You can't be sure of that. Someone else might have taken your place.

ADRIAN. When I was at Loch Leven——

ARTHUR. I got a three-and-a-half pounder on this fellow in Orkney two years ago.

ADRIAN (*coldly*). You've told me about that.

DENYS. You've most successfully worked the conversation round from where we started.

MIRANDA (*rising and moving to the front of the fire*). Because I'd rather not talk about Rowena.

DENYS (*rising to face her*). You've been made too much of in this family in the past and you resent any competition—that's what's the matter with you. Especially when the competitor's looks put your little monkey-face in the shade.

MIRANDA (*furiously*). I may have a monkey face, but at least my hair—and my face—is natural, which is more than hers are.

ADRIAN. Scissors ? Where are they ?

DENYS. You never powder your nose, do you ?

ARTHUR. On the mantelpiece. (*He rises and crosses* R. *for them.*)

MIRANDA. Of course I do, but I don't go to bed with my head like a sausage machine !

ARTHUR (*to* DENYS *as he passes between them*). Excuse me. (*He takes the scissors from the mantelpiece and goes back to the table.*)

DENYS. Sausage machine ? What d'you mean ?

MIRANDA. Just what I say. She's all screwed up in curlers. You'd get a nasty shock if there was a fire in the middle of the night.

DENYS (*horror-stricken*). *Curlers ?* I don't believe you.

MIRANDA (*crossing to up* C.). Start a fire, then, and see. (*She goes to the window.*)

(DENYS *breaks to the fireplace, then turns. He is disturbed.*)

ADRIAN. Two useful dry flies. A Greenwell's Glory and——

ARTHUR. A Red Quill. Very useful. Are those mine ?
(*Taking them.*)

ADRIAN. No, they are not. (*Taking them back.*)

ARTHUR. Sorry.

DENYS (*crossing up to* MIRANDA). Nobody wears *curlers*
nowadays.

MIRANDA (*slightly uneasy at the effect she has produced*). Don't
be silly, hundreds of people do.

DENYS (*suddenly*). You're a nasty little cat, aren't you ?

MIRANDA. Yes. I suppose I am.

DENYS (*turning away to face down stage, and filling his pipe*).
You know—that's the sort of thing a man would be incapable of
saying about another man.

MIRANDA. I should hope so.

DENYS. You know what I mean all right.

MIRANDA. Well, taking a job simply because it was more
money, when it meant giving up the work I really wanted to do,
is something *I'd* be incapable of doing.

DENYS (*moving down the steps to* R. *and sitting on the* L. *arm of
the chair above the fire*). Oh, for God's sake, shut up about the
wretched job.

MIRANDA (*on the steps up* C.). I won't shut up. For years I've
—admired you and looked up to you—you know I have. I've done
things and I haven't done things because I thought you'd've
approved or disapproved. You only went as Paul Perry's
secretary because it gave you time to work at your drawing and
designing, you know you did. You should have stuck to law if
all you meant to be was somebody's lap-dog secretary. You
must have developed very expensive tastes suddenly, for you
hadn't much to live on then. And in spite of the fact that
everyone disapproved you were successful. I sat in the gallery
at " Tiger in Mayfair " and nearly clapped my hands off when
the curtain went up on each scene—you got a round on *nearly*
every one, though I did clap once all by myself. If Rowena was
worth tuppence nothing would induce her to let you give it all
up.

DENYS. Miranda—I'm only going to America . . .

MIRANDA. I'm not saying a bit what I meant to say, but I'm
saying what I mean. If you go with Paul Perry I shall—I
shall—— (*Suddenly near tears.*) I'm going to make some
toffee.

(*She dashes out* L.)

ARTHUR (*looking up*). What was all that about ?

DENYS (*crossing up to the bay*). God knows.

(*He goes out into the garden.*)

ADRIAN. She's going to make some toffee. When I was at Loch Leven——

ARTHUR (*checking him*). While we're alone—about to-night.

ADRIAN. But surely there's been too much rain ? We can't——

ARTHUR. Of course we can. An afternoon's rain is nothing. Are you funking it ?

ADRIAN. Not funking it, exactly, but——

ARTHUR. Good. Pecker says ten o'clock is as early as we should be there. He's arranged the meeting place——

(MILDRED *enters and they both start guiltily.*)

MILDRED (*crossing up to the garden door*). Parsley.

(*She goes out.*)

ARTHUR. Did you bring a macintosh ?

ADRIAN. Yes, but——

ARTHUR. And you've got thick boots on ?

ADRIAN. Yes, but——

ARTHUR. Then you're ready.

ADRIAN. As far as clothing's concerned—yes. But I'm worried, Arthur, and it's no good pretending I'm not. I'm on the Bench next week. I shouldn't do it. Just supposing anything went wrong ?

ARTHUR. But that's all been thought out. Tom Mace, the Water Bailiff, has a fruity tenor voice and he's singing in the concert. All his satellites will be there to hear him—he makes them go, Pecker says——

ADRIAN. But——

ARTHUR. Wait a minute—there's always a bun-fight afterwards and that should keep him busy until about eleven. By that time we'll either be home—or on our way home.

(MILDRED *enters from the garden door.*)

MILDRED (*crossing to the house door from the garden with some parsley*). I can't think what a centipede wants with so many legs.

(*She goes out L.*)

ARTHUR. So there's nothing to worry about. (*Picking up a cast.*) Where did you get this ?

ADRIAN. Martins. I was just going to tell you, when I was at Loch Leven——

(BELLA *enters with a cloth from* L.)

BELLA. I'm sorry, but I'll have to clear you off the table, sir. I'll have to get set.

ARTHUR (*rising*). Right you are, Bella. (*Picking up his*

casts.) Take yours, Adrian, before I snaffle them. (*He moves up into the bay.*)

(ADRIAN *rises, collecting his casts, etc.*)

ADRIAN (*to below the steps*). It's been very interesting, very interesting indeed. But I must tell you about when I was at——

ARTHUR (*looking out of the window*). Mary! (*Stepping through the garden door.*) I'd go round, the grass is soaking.

(BELLA *is spreading the tablecloth.*)

MARY (*calling, off*). Right! I will.

ARTHUR (*returning*). What were you saying about Loch Leven ?

ADRIAN. Oh, yes, I—what was it ? I can't remember. When I was at Loch Leven I—it was something I did—or used——

ARTHUR. Perhaps you'll remember later on.

(BELLA *goes out* L. ADRIAN *absently puts his things, including a small oil bottle, down on the cloth again.*)

ADRIAN. Was—Mary coming here ?

ARTHUR (*on the rostrum up* C.). Yes. She's going to the concert with Mildred.

ADRIAN. Don't leave me alone with her, Arthur.

ARTHUR. But I thought that was what you wanted ?

ADRIAN. Yes, it is, but—oh well, perhaps it might be a good idea. I don't know——

(MILDRED *enters with salad in a bowl.*)

MILDRED. Arthur, it's gone wrong again. (*Glancing upward.*) Go up and see to it, will you ? (*She moves to the* L. *end of the table.*)

ARTHUR. Bother the thing.

MILDRED. And *will* you take this rubbish off the table ! Ach ! That greasy bottle on my good cloth——

ADRIAN (*seizing it*). I'm so sorry——

MILDRED. Are they yours ? It's quite all right. I thought they were Arthur's. (*She goes down* L. *to the dresser.*)

ARTHUR (*coming down—crossing*). Mary's on her way round.

MILDRED. Is she ?

(ARTHUR *goes out* L. MILDRED *returns to the table with knives and forks.*)

Have you said anything to her, Adrian ?

ADRIAN. No. I just sit dumb and paralysed when she's in the room. Or else chatter like an idiot.

MILDRED. Well, you can't expect to get very far, then, can you ?

ADRIAN. But don't you think that if there'd been any hope— well, I mean, she'd have given me a sign ? Some encouragement ?

MILDRED. But if you've been sitting dumb and paralysed you might not have noticed if she had.

ADRIAN. I think I should. I've always felt that the actual proposal shouldn't be necessary if both parties—I mean, there should be a something—(*sawing the air backwards and forwards*) between them.

MILDRED. And you don't feel there's any of (*doing the same with knives in her hands*) that between you ?

ADRIAN. I'm afraid not.

MILDRED. I'm sure I don't know what to suggest. The ordinary method seemed quite satisfactory in my own case. Arthur said, " Will you marry me ? " and I said, " Yes. When ? " (*Setting out the knives and forks.*)

ADRIAN. Wasn't that a little—well, bald ?

MILDRED (*crossing* L. *to the dresser*). We added a few embroideries afterwards, but at least it was quite clear.

ADRIAN. I don't believe all women would like it.

MILDRED (*returning to the table with the silver, etc.*). Now, Adrian, what do you know about women ? Stop trying to be a psychologist and get on with it.

ADRIAN. I don't want to spoil everything by rushing things.

MILDRED. A little rushing might make a pleasant change, don't you think ?

ADRIAN (*sitting at* R. *of the table. Sententiously*). Women have to be wooed——

(MILDRED *sets the table.*)

MILDRED. Then go on, woo her. Oh, Adrian, don't use such silly words. I'd like to think of Mary living in our old house, with you.

ADRIAN. So would I.

MILDRED. Her own may be very old and quaint, but the plumbing's even older and quainter. She'd be much more comfortable with you at Whiteways.

ADRIAN. That's an idea.

MILDRED. What is ?

(MARY *enters at the door* L. ADRIAN *rises.*)

MARY. Has Arthur hanged himself ?

MILDRED. I don't think so.

MARY. His legs are dangling through the manhole in a most upsetting way.

MILDRED (*crossing* L.). Isn't that like him! He's mending the wrong thing. Excuse me. (*Opening the door.*) Arthur! (*Going out.*) It isn't the *bath* plug——

(*She exits* L. *A pause.* ADRIAN *is rather confused. Bus.*)

MARY. Well, the rain's stopped. Isn't that a blessing? (*She sits in the armchair* L.)

ADRIAN. Yes. Yes, it is. (*He sits on the chair* R. *of the table.*)

MARY. But I suppose, being a fisherman, you welcome a little rain?

ADRIAN. Yes. At least, a certain amount.

MARY. I'm afraid I don't. My house is very damp. I suppose that is the price of age.

(*She is toying with things in her bag and not looking at him. A pause.*)

ADRIAN (*rises—suddenly*). Mary, can I speak to you?

MARY (*taken aback*). Well—aren't you?

ADRIAN (*moving* C., *above the table*). Yes, but I mean rather specially.

MARY. What is it?

ADRIAN. I hope you won't mind—I mean, that you won't consider I'm being too blunt, or anything?

MARY. I'm sure I won't.

ADRIAN. Well—— (*A pause. Suddenly.*) You like my house, don't you?

MARY. Very much.

ADRIAN. It is a nice house. Let me see . . . Your house has no bathroom, has it?

MARY. No, but I'm having one put in, you know.

ADRIAN. Don't do that. I shouldn't do that if I were you. It's a very costly business. I have a lovely bathroom on the first floor and another small one at the top.

MARY. It's very kind of you, but although our gardens are adjoining, I think it's rather a long way to run in a dressing-gown.

ADRIAN. But, dear me, I didn't mean that. I thought that —just possibly—*my* house might be, well—more convenient for you . . . (*Trailing away.*)

MARY. But, Adrian, I didn't know you were——

ADRIAN. Nobody did until I told Arthur yesterday, and he told me I'd better—tell you. I was afraid it would be no good.

MARY. It isn't. I'm so sorry. You see, I'm really very fond of my funny little place in spite of all its inconveniences. So I think I shall stay there, for the present, anyway. But on the other hand, I'm sure you'll easily find someone who would love——

ADRIAN. No, no. Just anyone won't do. You're *quite*
sure——

MARY. Quite.

ADRIAN. Then let's say no more about it. (*He sits on the
chair above the table.*)

MARY. Very well.

(*A pause.*)

ADRIAN. I wish I wasn't so dull.

MARY. But you're not, Adrian.

ADRIAN. I can't sparkle or be witty. I've tried—it's quite
hopeless. The most anyone can say of me is that I'm never
deliberately unkind. Have you ever thought, Mary, how very
sad it is to go through life with that the best anyone can say of
you ?

MARY (*rising, and to him*). But I'm sure you're wrong. I've
often heard Arthur say what an excellent companion you were.

ADRIAN (*eagerly*). Have you ? How very nice of him.
(*Deflating.*) But I'm afraid that's just because we have so many
interests in common. And because I don't talk at the wrong
time. I remember Arthur once saying to me on a nasty Channel
crossing, " Thank God, Adrian, you don't talk ! "

MARY. That's a very valuable asset.

ADRIAN. Perhaps it is. Though actually when he said it I
was quite incapable of speech.

MARY. You know, I think you're suffering from a mild attack
of liver—or you need a holiday. Why don't you try doing
something different for a change ?

ADRIAN. I'm very conservative.

MARY. Much too conservative.

(ROWENA *enters* L., *carrying a letter.*)

ROWENA. Thank heavens, it seems to have stopped raining.
Does anyone know how far Millmere is from here ?

ADRIAN (*still seated*). About twenty miles, I suppose.

ROWENA (*at* L.C.). Is that all ? Are you sure ?

ADRIAN. It might be twenty-five. It can't be more.

ROWENA. I must tell Denys. D'you know where he is ?

ADRIAN (*rising and moving up into the bay*). In the garden, I
believe.

ROWENA (*moving to the garden door*). I was asked to a cocktail
party there to-night, and we might go if that's all it is.

(*She goes out to the garden calling " Denys ! " as she catches sight
of him.*)

MARY (*rising*). Are you going to the concert ? (*She moves
up to* R. *of the* L. *pillar.*)

ADRIAN. No, I'm not. I only wish I was. I'm going—fishing with Arthur.

(*He sits in the window seat.* MARY *joins him.* ARTHUR *enters* L.)

ARTHUR. I think I've settled its hash effectively this time.

(MILDRED *enters with a jug of cream which she puts on the table, followed by* MIRANDA *with the cruet, etc.*)

MILDRED (*above the table*). I won't be a minute, Mary, I'm just going up to change. Arthur, be a dear and fill the coal bucket. Bella's making to-morrow's tart.

(*She goes out as* ROWENA *and* DENYS *enter from the garden.* ARTHUR *moves up* L.)

ROWENA (*to above the table, addressing* ARTHUR). Will anyone mind if we go to see some friends of mine instead of going to the concert ?

ARTHUR (*up* L.C. *by the banister*). Not in the least.

ROWENA. Quite sure ? I don't want to offend anybody.

ARTHUR. We're not easily offended here.

(DENYS *moves to the armchair* L.)

ROWENA (*to* DENYS). Are you ready ?

DENYS (*sitting on the arm of the chair* L.). As ready as I can be. I can't dress up because another pair of flannel bags is all I've got.

ROWENA. Heavens ! Nobody dresses up for Elena's. I'll get a coat.

(*She exits* L. *A pause.*)

MIRANDA (L. *of the table, turning to* DENYS). Aren't you coming to the concert ?

DENYS. No. They can warble undisturbed by my ribald mirth.

(MIRANDA *looks stricken.*)

Don't worry, you'll have a packed house, they always do. Most of the others are going.

MIRANDA. I know.

ARTHUR. Marcia and Jim are meeting you there.

(ROWENA *enters* L. MIRANDA *turns away above and* R. *of the table.*)

ROWENA. I'm ready.

(DENYS *rises.*)

ARTHUR (*above end* L.C. *of the table*). Are you coming back to supper ?

DENYS. I should think so.

ROWENA. I shouldn't. Elena's cocktail etceteras are a supper in themselves. Just expect us when you see us.

MIRANDA. Good-bye. I do hope you enjoy yourselves. (*To* ROWENA.) Are you quite sure you'll be warm enough ?

ROWENA (*surprised*). Quite, thank you.

DENYS (*grinning*). But thank you so much for asking. Good luck at the concert.

MIRANDA. Thank *you*.

DENYS (*to* ROWENA). Mind the step.

(*He exits with* ROWENA. MIRANDA *sits on the steps looking after them wistfully. After a pause she crosses up to the windows.*)

MARY (*taking out her cigarette case*). D'you smoke yet, Miranda ?

MIRANDA. No, thank you. Would you say that I was civil to Rowena just now ?

MARY. Very civil indeed.

MIRANDA. Then I'm a good actress, because I think she's the stupidest, selfishest woman alive.

ADRIAN. That's rather sweeping——

ARTHUR. I wouldn't go quite as far as that.

MARY. Don't you worry, Miranda——

MIRANDA (*chokily*). I'm not worrying, but I'd like to trample on her in hobnailed boots.

(*She goes out into the garden.*)

ADRIAN. Dear me——

MARY (*moving down to the edge of the rostrum*). Seventeen can be a heartbreaking age. Especially when your Secret Passion deserts you for someone else and a cocktail party.

ARTHUR (*moving to* R.C.). She seemed to be having a free fight with her Secret Passion earlier in the evening.

ELLA (*calling, off stage* L.). Mildred !

(ELLA SPENDER *rushes in* L., *followed by* SALLY.)

Mildred—(*tripping on the step.*) Bother the step. Be careful, Sally. (*To* L, *of* ARTHUR.) Oh, Arthur, have you anything in pots that would help to hide some dreadful boxes ? Or an old bedspread, or anything ?

ARTHUR. There's rather a difference——

ELLA. Forgive me (*to* MARY) for rushing in like this, but they've enlarged the stage with wooden boxes from the grocer's, and it's very awkward when Miss Willoughby's so absolutely enormous

MARY. Are you afraid she'll go through ?

ELLA. Yes, but it isn't that. The only ones the right size are marked in large letters on all four sides : PURE

VEGETABLE FAT! Isn't it teasing? I might find it funny if I wasn't in charge of the affair, but as it is it's bad enough that she's singing "Only God Can Make A Tree." Where's Mildred?

ARTHUR. Upstairs changing. Shall I tell her?

ELLA. No, don't bother, I'll go up myself and see if I can find anything. Wait here, Sally. (*Crossing up* L.) This *could* only happen to me. Anyone else would have found plain boxes —mind the step.

(*She goes out* L., *calling* "Mildred!" SALLY *sits in the chair* L., *complacently.*)

MARY (*to* SALLY). I believe Miranda's in the garden, Sally.

SALLY. Is she?

(*There is a pause.*)

ARTHUR. Well . . . has anything exciting happened in Throppleton this week?

SALLY (*suddenly*). Yes! I fell into a vat of fish manure on Wednesday.

ADRIAN. Good heavens! (*He rises.*)

SALLY. I smelt very peculiar afterwards.

ARTHUR. I'm sure you did.

(*A pause :* ARTHUR *appeals silently to* MARY.)

MARY. Well, shall we go out and look for Miranda?

SALLY (*rising*). I've got my best things on.

MARY. We should be all right if we stick to the paths.

(SALLY *joins her in the bay.*)

Good gracious, the sun's actually trying to shine.

(*They go out by the garden door.*)

ARTHUR (*breaking* R.). Extraordinary what a paralysing effect a child can have on conversation.

ADRIAN (*miserably, coming down* L. *of* ARTHUR). Arthur, I've been thinking—about to-night——

ARTHUR. Now don't start all that over again. Buck up! Where's your adventurous spirit, man?

ADRIAN. I haven't got one.

ARTHUR. I'll give you a stiff whisky before we go out and perhaps you'll develop one. I'm going to enjoy myself. (*Moving to* R. *of the settee and sitting on it.*)

ADRIAN. I'm not. (*He moves to behind the settee—pauses— then suddenly.*) Of course it would be a new experience, wouldn't it? Something I've never done before.

(MIRANDA *appears at the garden windows and comes to* L. *of the bay.*)

And poaching *is* adventurous.

ARTHUR. Very.

ADRIAN. All right, then. (*They shake hands on it.*) But I wish we hadn't to wait until ten o'clock, though.

ARTHUR (*facing down stage, not seeing* MIRANDA). We'll have to start about half-past nine at the latest. Sam's going up earlier with the gaffs, etcetera. It'll take us half an hour at least to get to the Mill pool——

(MIRANDA *comes down* L. *of the table.*)

MIRANDA (*accusingly*). Uncle Arthur !

(ARTHUR *rises.* ADRIAN *turns.*)

ARTHUR. What d'you mean—" Uncle Arthur ! " ?

MIRANDA. I heard. You're not going fishing at all——

ADRIAN. Sh ! Be quiet !

MIRANDA. I know what you're going to do. Oh, do take me with you. Please !

ADRIAN (*below the* R. *end of the table*). Certainly not—most certainly not.

(*They are below the table.*)

ARTHUR. You've got it all wrong——

MIRANDA. I haven't. I'll be as good as gold, I won't make a sound.

ARTHUR. No, Miranda, no.

ADRIAN. It isn't a woman's job.

MIRANDA. But I've always wanted to know how it's done.

ARTHUR. I shouldn't think you'd be likely to find out from us.

(*He crosses to the fire.* ADRIAN *breaks up* R.C. MARY *and* SALLY *enter from the garden.* MIRANDA *breaks a little* L.)

SALLY. I had to have two baths running, with lysol in the first and bath salts in the second.

MARY (*with relief*). And here's Miranda.

MIRANDA (*turning*). Hello !

SALLY (*coming down to* L.C.). Hello !

MIRANDA (*moving a step to* SALLY). D'you know your words ?

SALLY. Yes, but I feel awfully giggly.

MARY. Arthur ! The coals !

ARTHUR (*to the fireplace, seizing the bucket as* MILDRED'S *voice is heard*). My goodness, yes !

(*He makes for the garden door and exits as* MILDRED *enters* L., *followed by* ELLA SPENDER, *carrying a counterpane.* ADRIAN *moves to the chair below the fire.* MILDRED *to* C. *above the table.* ELLA *at* L.C.)

ELLA. This will do splendidly for one half and I'll use the nursery tablecloth for the other—they should cover most of the trouble. Thank you, Mildred, a thousand times. I must get across to the hall—there's so much to do—and the unreserveds will be going in. (*Turning.*) Sally darling, slip up to the house and get the nursery tablecloth for me—there's a dear !

SALLY. I'm always slipping here, and slipping there, and you can't slip upwards, anyway.

ELLA. Don't be silly. Oh, I think I'd better go myself. You're sure to bring the wrong one. Bring her with you, Mildred, will you ? And keep her clean if you can. Don't look at my hat, I know it's appalling. Luckily it's worse for you than me—I can't see it. You won't desert me at the end, Mildred ? You'll stay for a cup of quite undrinkable tea ?

MILDRED. Of course we will.

ELLA. Thank goodness ! Now behave nicely, Sally—oh, child ! What *do* you do to yourself ? (*Tweaking her coat.*) Why can't you look like the Henderson girl ? Neat and smart ?

SALLY (L.C.). That's easy. Because she has her clothes tailored for her, while I have to wear remnants made up by Miss McThomas.

ELLA (*to* MILDRED). It's quite true.

SALLY. She makes everything what she calls " to allow." Even my butterfly dress doesn't fit anywhere.

ELLA. I know it's awful, but never mind, dear, it's a very pretty dance.

SALLY. It's bad enough having to be a blasted butterfly at my age.

ELLA. Don't use that word, Sally, please ! I must fly. See you all later. Hold yourself straight, Sally, that helps a bit. Don't be long.

MILDRED. Mind the step.

ELLA. Oh, thank you. I was just going not to.

(MARY *has drifted to up* L.C. ELLA *goes out.* SALLY *goes to the armchair* L.)

MILDRED. I should think we might as well go. I like to be in time for everything.

(*As* ARTHUR *appears at the garden door with the coal, slapping his face.*)

Thank you, Arthur. Put some on the fire, will you ?

ARTHUR (*crossing down to the fireplace*). Mildred, where's your beastly midge stuff ?

MILDRED. On my dressing-table, marked not to be taken. Miranda, would you——

MIRANDA (*below the armchair* L.). I'll try.

(*She exits* L.)

MILDRED.   That child's too docile to be healthy at the moment.
ARTHUR.   Anything is better than being eaten alive.
ADRIAN.   I could do with some myself.

(*Enter* BELLA, *with the veal-and-ham pie, wearing her hat and coat.*)

BELLA (L. *of the table*).   The pie has got bashed a bit on the journey, but I dare say it'll eat none the worse.   Now, is that everything ?

(MARY *crosses to below the door* L.)

MILDRED.   I think so.   Wait a minute, I'll give you your ticket.   Where's my bag ?   (*To the armchair* R.)   Here we are.
BELLA.   And what about the key ?
MILDRED (*at* C. *above the table*).   Put it under the flower-pot and the last person brings it in.

(ARTHUR *is at the fire.*)

ADRIAN (*seated below the fireplace*).   How do you know whether you're the last person or not ?
ARTHUR (*moving to up* R.C.).   Leave the garden door unlocked. There's nothing to steal, anyway.
MILDRED.   Very well.   You take the key, then, Bella.   And that's your ticket, I hope you enjoy it.
BELLA (*taking the ticket*).   Thank you.   You always get a laugh, that's one thing—whether it's meant or not.   I'll lock up at the back.

(*She turns and goes out* L.)

MILDRED (*crossing to the fire*).   Have your suppers when you like, Arthur, but don't eat all the egg out of the salad.   If we've forgotten anything, fish for it in the larder.

(MIRANDA *enters* L. *and moves to* C.)

MIRANDA.   Is this it ?   (*Holding out a bottle to* ARTHUR.)
ARTHUR (*moving to her*).   I'll know when you get within a yard of me.   (*He takes the bottle.*)   Yes, it is.
SALLY (*going to the sideboard*).   Can I have a drink of lemonade ?
MARY (*pouring it out*).   I'm sure you can.
MILDRED (*putting coal on the fire*).   Have you got everything you need, Miranda ?
MIRANDA.   Yes, I just wear this for the sketch.
ARTHUR (*moving towards* MILDRED).   I was just going to do that——
MILDRED (*turning at the fire*).   Now let's get this quite clear once and for all, Arthur.   You were *not*.   I always ask you to, because it keeps up the fiction that you sometimes do it before

our guests.   But if I didn't do it, it would be out long before you
did anything.

(ARTHUR *helps* MILDRED *on with her coat.*)

SALLY (*at the sideboard*).   Ugh !   This is Mother's recipe with
the Epsom's Salts in.   They simply come up and hit you.

MILDRED.   Not if you don't know they're in.   Be quiet.
(*Crossing to* L.C.)   Arthur, did you remember to trim the lamps ?

ARTHUR (*moving to* C.).   I'll do them before we go.

MILDRED.   Don't forget.

(ADRIAN *rises and moves to* R.C.)

MARY.   We'd better go down the road, I think.   It's quicker.

MILDRED (*crossing* MIRANDA, *to the door* L.).   The bread's in
the bin, Arthur, and don't use the new loaf—it's for to-morrow.

ARTHUR.   Go on.   We'll be all right.

MIRANDA (*aside*).   Good luck for to-night.

MILDRED (*at the door*).   And *don't* forget the lamps.   Oh !
Did anyone bring the chairs in ?—Of course, they're not out.
Good-bye.

(MARY *goes out, followed by* SALLY *and* MILDRED *and* MIRANDA.)

ARTHUR (*putting the midge stuff on his face*).   Peace, at last.

(ADRIAN *follows suit.*)

ADRIAN (*suddenly*).   Arthur, do Water Bailiffs use blood-
hounds ?

ARTHUR.   I don't think so.   Why ?

ADRIAN (*sniffing*).   Because if they do—we're for it !

CURTAIN.

SCENE 2

SCENE.—*The same as Act II, Scene 1.   Several hours later the
same night.*

When the CURTAIN *rises the stage is in darkness, but two figures are
dimly discernible in the firelight,* DENYS *and* ROWENA.

ROWENA (*groping her way towards the fire*).   Well, there's no
point in sulking.   I'm sorry you didn't enjoy yourself.   I did.
(*She is now near the fireplace.*)

DENYS (*lighting the lamp on the* L. *pillar*).   That was obvious.

ROWENA.   It was just as obvious that you didn't.   As a
matter of fact you were exceedingly rude.

DENYS.   Be thankful I wasn't even ruder.

ROWENA   I know Charlie's a half-wit, but you might at least
have listened. when he tried to tell you about Hollywood.

Denys (*sitting on the back of the settee facing* o., *away from* Rowena). Charlie was more than half-seas-over and I couldn't see that listening to his amorous adventures in Hollywood or anywhere else could possibly benefit either him or me.

Rowena. You've gone very puritanical all of a sudden. (*She flops in the armchair above the fire.*)

Denys. After a party like that I feel like becoming a rabid teetotaller and asking Mother to look out a few antimacassars.

Rowena. I told you it was a cocktail party.

Denys. But you didn't say anything about a petting party, or that it was to go on half the night.

Rowena. I've been to parties with you before now that weren't exactly Quaker Meetings.

Denys. I dare say, but you've never been to one like to-night's with me before—and you never will again.

Rowena. You're quite right there. (*Yawning.*) Oh dear, oh dear, I'm sleepy! After to-night I thought you wouldn't object if I arranged to be called for here to-morrow ?

Denys. Not at all.

Rowena. I dare say I'm being rude now, but I'll think up some excuse for Mrs. Royd.

Denys. I shouldn't bother.

Rowena. No, I'm sure you wouldn't, but I will. (*Rising.*) Oh well, to-night's settled things definitely, and it's probably a very good thing. You can go back to your daubing and peculiar angles in peace.

Denys. Thank you.

Rowena. And to your baby-snatching.

(Denys *rises and turns.*)

Sorry—rather a cheap jibe. I take it back ! But if you *do* decide to go to America, I should watch your behaviour. American hostesses might not be so forbearing as Elena was to-night. Good night. (*She crosses* Denys *towards the door* L.)

Denys. Just a minute.

Rowena. What ?

Denys. I suppose I was damned rude this evening.

Rowena. You were.

Denys. If you like I'll write and apologize—say I had a headache. I don't know. I only know that the whole affair made me sick, but if you think it would make things easier for you, I'll——

Rowena. There's no need to. I'll tell Elena the headache story. What are you going to do about your damp bedclothes ?

Denys. I'll sleep in here and use my coat. That'll give the family a chance to say " I told you so " in the morning.

Rowena. You couldn't know the tent leaked.

Denys. I might have looked to see.

Rowena. Well, you've got a nice fire. 'Bye-'bye. It was very pleasant while it lasted. 'Night. (*She crosses to the door.*)
Denys. Good night.

(Rowena *exits* L. Denys *puts some coal on the fire, then goes up, and opens the garden door and breathes deeply.* Rowena *re-enters, carrying bedclothes.*)

Rowena. Denys!
Denys (*at the banister*). Yes?
Rowena. The angel-child isn't in bed.
Denys. D'you mean Miranda?
Rowena. Yes.
Denys. Are you sure? (*Glancing at the clock.*)
Rowena. Quite. Unless she's gone amazingly thin and carefully arranged herself under the mattress.
Denys. She's probably stayed the night with the Spenders. She was going there after the concert.
Rowena. Then what about you having her bedclothes?
Denys. That's an idea.
Rowena. Much as I may have hated you to-night, I didn't like the thought of you shivering in the dawn.
Denys. I suppose they *have* come back? (*Coming down the steps to* c.)
Rowena. Yes. Your brother-in-law's snoring and I heard someone turn over in your mother's room. The mattress squeaks. Here you are.
Denys (*taking the bedclothes*). Thank you.
Rowena. Not at all. A few coals of fire to keep you warm. Good night.

(*She turns away and exits* L. Denys *puts the bedclothes on the chair* R. *of the table. He wanders up to the garden door and locks it. Returning to* c., *he takes off his coat and his collar and tie and then goes out* L. *In a few seconds he returns in a dressing-gown, and putting the bedclothes on the settee, he turns out the lamp. Then he lights a cigarette, and lying down on the settee, smokes, looking into the fire. He flings the cigarette away and is just settling down, when a scrabbling noise comes from the garden door.* Denys *sits up, faintly illuminated by the firelight. The garden door is vigorously shaken.*)

Denys (*rising*). Half a minute.

(*The noise stops.* Denys *crosses quickly up to the garden door and opens it. There appears to be no one there.*)

Who's there?

(Miranda *appears in the doorway.*)

MIRANDA. Oh, thank goodness it's you. Who locked the door ?

DENYS. I did.

(MIRANDA *moves to the centre of the bay.*)

MIRANDA (*as he is about to do so again*). Don't lock it.

DENYS. Why not ?

MIRANDA (*giggling*). There's someone else to come.

DENYS (*on her* L.). What d'you mean ? Look here, what are you doing, out at this time of night ? Do you know it's nearly one o'clock ?

MIRANDA. Is it ? I've been—fishing with Uncle Arthur and Mr. Barasford. Uncle Arthur hasn't come back, has he ?

DENYS. I don't know. I've only just got back myself.

MIRANDA. Then he hasn't. (*Coming down to* L.C.) If you've only just come in you can't talk to me about being late !

DENYS. There's a considerable difference in our ages.

MIRANDA. I know. Eleven years and one month, to be exact.

DENYS (*coming down to* R. *of* MIRANDA). Why didn't you come home with Father, if this story's true ?

MIRANDA. I couldn't—or *he* couldn't. I'm thinner than he is. Oh Denys, we've had the most exciting night. I might as well tell you because Uncle Arthur's bound to be here soon and you'll have to know.

DENYS. Know what ?

MIRANDA (*suddenly*). Unless—— (*She darts up to the garden door and looks out.*) Denys, supposing they caught him !

DENYS. Caught Father ? Who ? What on earth are you talking about ?

MIRANDA (*returning to down* L.C.). We've been poaching salmon and the Water Bailiffs caught us at it.

DENYS. *What ! !*

MIRANDA. Uncle Arthur had a bet with Mr. Barasford that he couldn't get a salmon first go.

DENYS. I don't believe you. Old Barasford *poaching salmon* ?

MIRANDA. Uncle Arthur was to do the poaching and he just had to be there to see fair play.

DENYS. And they took you ?

MIRANDA (*crossing to sit in the chair* L.). No, they didn't. I just went. I slipped out after we came home and joined them. And I was very useful. I held the light when they got it.

DENYS. But—my God ! D'you mean they actually got a *fish* ? (*He moves down* R. *of, and below the table.*)

MIRANDA. Of course they did. It was a beauty ! There wasn't time to weigh it though, because the men arrived. There was just time for Sam to say : " Get down the river—I'll lead

them up " and Uncle Arthur said, " For God's sake, run ! "—
and I ran.

DENYS. What happened to Barasford ?

MIRANDA. Well, somebody went into the river, but it might
have been Sam Pecker, I couldn't see. I lost Uncle Arthur in
a wood where he couldn't push under a fallen tree. It was just
like being on the films. I don't know *what* I'm going to do with
these shorts. Nobody would have been surprised a year or so
ago, but I can't think how to explain them now.

DENYS. Miranda, are you sure you haven't dreamt it all ?

MIRANDA. Quite certain. (*Rising, to him.*) Feel my shorts.

DENYS. They are soaking.

MIRANDA. I crawled a considerable way through a bog. I
hope your girl friend's asleep, or she'll wonder a bit, won't she ?

DENYS (*pulling his dressing-gown off*). I don't think she'll be
asleep yet—not that she'd care. Here, take your shorts off and
put this on. I'll get you a hot whisky—you can change while
I put the kettle on.

MIRANDA (*crossing to the fire*). Don't make a noise or Bella'll
wake. You'd better bring it in here.

DENYS (*going out*). Be quick, then.

(MIRANDA *slips her shorts off and puts on* DENYS's *dressing-gown.*
Off L. *the sound of a running tap is heard.*)

(*Re-entering.*) Those damned taps make the hell of a noise.
Bella stopped snoring—but she started again.

MIRANDA. The fire's not bad. Did you bring plenty for
Uncle Arthur ? I have a feeling he'll need some.

DENYS (*crossing to the fire and putting the kettle on it*). This is
the first time I'll have had the pleasure of reversing the usual
father and son position. I mean to make the most of it.

MIRANDA (*anxiously*). I only hope you'll have the chance to.
(*Crouching down in front of the fire.*) Oh, Denys, it was priceless !
You should have seen Uncle Arthur and Mr. Barasford hanging
over the bank with Sam giving orders and getting furious because
Mr. Barasford's foot slipped, and then going for me because I
wasn't holding the light properly—I got so excited I took the
light right off the fish—but only for a second. (*She sneezes.*)
It's all right—I often sneeze.

DENYS (*sitting on the chair below the fire*). Who won the bet ?
Old Barasford, I suppose ?

MIRANDA. I'm not sure. Once the fish was on the bank
every one seemed to be shouting at once. I dropped the flare in
the water by mistake and the fish was thrashing about in the
dark with Sam and Mr. Barasford after it on their hands and
knees. Before that Mr. Barasford had been moaning and
groaning and wanting to go home.

DENYS. I bet he had——

MIRANDA. But once it was caught, he was bobbing about shouting : " We'll lose him ! Do something ! " and then Sam found his flashlight, got it and killed it, and he was whooping with joy and excitement so I don't wonder they found us.

(*She sneezes again.* DENYS *rises and gives her the bedclothes.*)

DENYS. Here, put this round you, and the moment you've had your whisky you're going to bed. These, by the way, are your bedclothes. I thought you must be staying at the Spenders when Rowena said you weren't in bed. (*He sits at the* L. *end of the settee.*)

(MIRANDA *wraps the eiderdown round her.*)

MIRANDA. Oh ! So she told you, did she ? Of course—you went to a party. Did you enjoy yourself ?

DENYS (*after a short pause*). Yes, thank you.

MIRANDA. Well, that was nice for you.

DENYS. How did the concert go ?

MIRANDA. Very well—on the whole. Sally giggled in the middle of our duologue, but it didn't matter much. Tell me all you did. Did you play games, or did people sing, or what ?

DENYS. Everyone sat about talking a lot of rot, and getting amorous and drinking too much.

MIRANDA. Oh ! I didn't know it was going to be that sort of party.

DENYS. Neither did I.

(*A pause.*)

MIRANDA. Denys !

DENYS. Yes ?

MIRANDA. I'm—I'm sorry for half the things I said this afternoon—and I do wish I hadn't told you about—about the curlers. It was so unfair, in a way. I was in a temper and I hated her. And—actually she looks very nice because she ties a ribbon round them with a bow on the top——

DENYS. All right. Shut up about it.

MIRANDA. Are you horribly angry with me ?

DENYS. Pretty horribly.

MIRANDA. I wouldn't mind you being angry if it did any good—about your job, I mean.

DENYS (*dryly*). It's nice to know somebody's so interested.

MIRANDA. You shouldn't have talked to me so much about it if you didn't want me to be interested.

DENYS (*smiling*). I'm beginning to think I shouldn't.

(*Another pause.*)

MIRANDA. Denys !

DENYS. Yes ?

MIRANDA. If I ask you something terribly—impertinent, will you be very angry ?

DENYS. I expect so. (*He pauses.*) What is it ?

MIRANDA. Are you . . . are you *really* in l—— I daren't ask it.

DENYS. No. The answer is " no "—and she isn't with me.

MIRANDA. I knew that before.

DENYS. Did you indeed ? (*Rising and turning below the settee to* L.) The kettle should be hot enough now. (*He moves to the dresser for the whisky and a glass, taking the kettle with him.*)

MIRANDA (*rising*). Will you put some sugar in it, please ? (*To the edge of the settee.*) I hate whisky.

DENYS (*taking everything to the table* c.). Certainly, madam. I won't give you much. I wonder if we have any hot-water bottles in this establishment ?

MIRANDA (*moving to the fire*). I'm beautifully warm now. Put a spoon in the glass, then it won't crack.

DENYS. Is there anything you don't know, Miss Wise Child ?

MIRANDA. Quite a lot of things. Do you know how old I am ? I'm seventeen and a half.

DENYS (*crossing to her and sitting on the chair above the fire*). Practically in your dotage ! You look about fourteen and a half.

MIRANDA (*sitting at his feet*). That's only because you've known me so long. (*Suddenly.*) I wish this night could last for ever.

DENYS (*giving her the whisky*). Drink this, and go to bed.

MIRANDA. You've often taken me out, but I've never sat by a fire and talked to you like this before.

DENYS (*lightly*). No. You've always been too busy eating.

MIRANDA. And I don't suppose I ever will again.

DENYS. Go on, drink.

(MIRANDA *drinks. A pause.*)

What's the matter ?

MIRANDA (*gulping*). Nothing. (*Tremulously.*) It's just that it's awfully hot . . . (*She puts down the glass and turning her head away from him, rubs the sleeve of his coat across her eyes.*)

DENYS (*taking hold of her shoulders, and speaking gently*). What is it, you great baby ?

(MIRANDA *turns, and flinging her arms round his neck, buries her face in his shoulder, sobbing, and talking almost incoherently.*)

MIRANDA. Oh Denys, Denys !—I suppose I am just a child—I know you think I am—but I don't feel like one and I'm—— You'll go away and—and I'll—never see you again.

DENYS. Hush, sweetheart. (*He strokes her hair, looking worriedly over her shoulder.*)

MIRANDA. It doesn't matter whether you're a—a child or not. You can be just as—miserable—can't you ?

DENYS. Of course you can.

MIRANDA. I didn't know I *could* feel like this—but—I can——

(*A pause.*)

DENYS. Steady, darling. (*He pauses.*) Listen, Miranda darling, stop crying. I want to talk to you, and I can't when you're sobbing so—bumpily.

MIRANDA. I'm sorry—it's all right—I'm stopping. (*In a minute she stops, and sits back on her knees, wiping her eyes with her hands.*) I haven't—sobbed like that for—ages.

DENYS. Here, use the sheet. (*He hands her the sheet.*)

MIRANDA (*wiping her eyes with it*). Thank you.

DENYS. Not at all—it's your own.

MIRANDA. What were you going to say ?

DENYS. Drink your whisky, but don't let it make you more weepy. It has that effect on some people.

MIRANDA. I'm all right—now.

(*She is sitting on the floor between him and the fire and* DENYS *puts his arm round her shoulders which are still shaken occasionally by dying sobs.*)

Go on.

DENYS. I'm going a long way back to the time when I was seventeen.

MIRANDA. And a half. Ten and threequarter years ago.

DENYS. You know, in the twelve months that I was seventeen I fell in love three times.

MIRANDA. Not properly.

DENYS. No, but you see that's just the point, sweetheart. It's awfully difficult to know at that age whether it's properly or not.

MIRANDA. *I* know.

DENYS (*gently*). No, you don't. By properly, I mean here, now, and for ever more, until death us do part.

(MIRANDA *puts up her hand and takes hold of his.*)

You see, I find it difficult to know now—at my great age—and believe me, it's quite impossible to know at yours. I'm not saying that it makes things any easier at the time. I know it doesn't. But you've got to be very careful to remember that as you grow older your feelings for people change.

MIRANDA. I can't imagine changing.

DENYS. No one ever can, at the time. But people that you think you—love, you suddenly find you only have a very deep affection for instead, and that's a very different thing.

MIRANDA. I know it is.

DENYS. Sometimes there isn't even that left, so you see, "Love" is a word you've got to be very chary of using. Will you remember that ?

MIRANDA. Yes.

DENYS. I'm a queer one to be lecturing you, but I'd have behaved a lot more sensibly if I'd taken my own advice.

MIRANDA. Perhaps you will now.

DENYS. Perhaps, but I shouldn't count on it.

MIRANDA. Denys, can I say it just once, to you ?

DENYS. No. (*More gently.*) But thank you very much for wanting to.

MIRANDA. I shall some day. When I'm too old for you possibly to say I'm a child, I shall come and find you, wherever you are, and say it then. And even if you have a wife and a hundred children you won't be able to stop me—just to prove that you're wrong—in my case, because you are, you know.

DENYS. I wish I was as sure.

MIRANDA. Denys !——

DENYS (*rising*). Go to bed. Go on, it's high time——

(*A voice outside calls* "Coo-e-e." MIRANDA *catches sight of something out of the window.*)

MIRANDA (*rising quickly*). Who's that ? It's Uncle Arthur ! At least I hope it is.

(DENYS *darts to the garden door and opens it.* ADRIAN BARASFORD *comes in, dripping.*)

ADRIAN (*crossing* DENYS). I was just passing—I wondered if your father was in at all . . . (*To* R.C., *below the steps.*)

DENYS. Just a neighbourly call—at one a.m.

ADRIAN. Well——

MIRANDA (*above the top of the settee*). Oh heavens ! He isn't here, Mr. Barasford.

ADRIAN. Thank goodness, you are.

DENYS. Come in. I'll get you a whisky.

ADRIAN. No, no, please——

(DENYS *moves to* L. *of the table.*)

MIRANDA. Yes, come in. He knows about everything. I had to tell him. (*Handing him her glass.*) Take this. It isn't as hot as it might be, but we've got the kettle on. What happened to you ?

ADRIAN (*coming down* C., *to* R. *of the table*). I plunged into the river. By mistake, really, but once in, it seemed a good idea. I tried to walk across, but of course it was too deep. I had to swim and I got swept away by the current which was quite a good thing in a way. Oh, what an awful night ! I never had a nightmare as bad as this !

DENYS. I must say I never thought you'd have allowed yourself to be led so very far astray. I've always regarded you as a model of all the virtues.

ADRIAN. And so I was, so I was. At least, I mean (*he sits* R. *of the table*)—I can't think what came over me. D'you realize I'm on the Bench and I've poached a salmon ? I—a Justice of the Peace, have poached a salmon, and been very nearly caught doing so, what's more. (*He groans.*) Poor Sam Pecker ! I wonder what's happened to him ? The awful feeling of being pursued. I shall never hunt again. Just look at my trousers and this isn't really an old suit. I shall never live this down in my own memory. Never. I wonder what weight it really was ?

MIRANDA. Sam said twenty pounds. (*She moves to* c., *above the table.*)

ADRIAN. It's my belief it was more. But really, of course, what does it matter ? I had only one happy moment to-night. My sense of humour, which I'm afraid is not strong at any time, suddenly reared its head as I crawled through some particularly stubborn undergrowth and I thought how splendid it would be for me to be on the Bench when Arthur was brought up——

MIRANDA. You wretch !

ADRIAN. Well, he started all this. I pictured myself giving him a severe reprimand and a heavy fine—that I should have had to pay most of myself—and it struck me as amusing. But then a bramble smacked me across the face.

DENYS. And your sense of humour disappeared again ?

ADRIAN. It did. Oh dear, if Sam Pecker talks !

MIRANDA. He won't.

DENYS. If he does you can tell him you'll have him up with Father. After all, you're not in nearly such a serious position. Sam supplied the implements, Miranda held the light, and Father took the fish. (*He crosses* R. *to the fire with the kettle.*) You were just a spectator. You've got them in your pocket.

ADRIAN. Well—(*looking at* MIRANDA) not quite.

DENYS. Near enough.

(MIRANDA *is watching* DENYS. ARTHUR *silently opens the garden door,*)

ARTHUR (*in a gruff voice*). We've got you, Mr. Barasford. Come quietly !

(ADRIAN *with a squeak of fright, jumps out of his chair. The other two swing round.*)

MIRANDA. Oh, Uncle Arthur ! (*She backs to the fireplace and sits on the floor.*)

(ARTHUR *comes down to* C., *above the table.*)

DENYS. Father, renewing his youth.

ADRIAN (*moving up level with* ARTHUR). You silly ass!
Really! Most startling!

ARTHUR. Dear me! The nerves seem very jumpy to-night.
What's the matter with you all?

DENYS. You can't get away with that. I know everything.

ARTHUR. I expect you do. It's been a most interesting—and
revealing—experience. (*He moves down* L.)

ADRIAN. It's been dreadful, dreadful—and you know it has.

DENYS. I'd like to know where all this happened? (*He sits
on the chair below the fire.*)

ADRIAN (*above the table, pouring more whisky*). I haven't an
idea. Have you, Arthur?

ARTHUR. No, except that it was well above the mill. We
crawled miles before we found one.

ADRIAN (*breaking* R.). And we were just giving up——
Oh! (*pausing at* R.C.)—*Why* didn't we? Why had the wretched
thing to be just there? I shall never forgive myself. I shall
never go to the Old Boys' Dinner again. (*He moves down to the
fire with his whisky glass.*)

DENYS. What have the Old Boys got to do with it?

ARTHUR. That's where he made the bet.

ADRIAN. After the port.

ARTHUR. Well, you said it was easy, you proved your case
and won your bet.

ADRIAN (*kettle in hand*). I don't altogether agree with you
there. I think there's more skill in the business than I'd thought.
Sam Pecker himself said it was a brilliant strike. He could
hardly believe the fish was really on the bank.

ARTHUR. Ah, but the bet was " first attempt."

DENYS. You seem to be taking it very calmly.

ARTHUR. I have every reason to. (*Crossing to the sideboard.*)

DENYS. And supposing Adrian started a little quiet black-
mail?

ARTHUR (*bringing a glass to the table* C.). He could hardly do
that, considering he gaffed the fish.

DENYS. What!

ADRIAN (*pouring hot water into the whisky*). I'm afraid it's
true.

MIRANDA. I didn't tell you. Oh Denys, it was lovely.
Uncle Arthur couldn't get his feet wedged and Mr. Barasford
thought the fish was moving——

ADRIAN. It *was* moving.

ARTHUR (*breaking* L.). Nonsense——

ADRIAN. It *was*, there wasn't a moment to be lost, so I——
I——

ARTHUR (*below the armchair* L.). So he gaily gaffed it with a
spare gaff he had in his hand—right under my very nose.

ADRIAN (*putting the kettle down*). And from a very difficult, slanting angle, too. (*He seizes the poker and mounts the settee, demonstrating over the back.*) It was a long reach from my position, and you see Arthur was in my way here. " Over and up, with a good firm stroke," that's what Sam Pecker said, and that's just what I did. The weight was enormous, of course, but if you get him properly that doesn't matter, and those things have a barb on the end which is a help, but still it must be done properly. And I flatter myself I did do it properly. I stood, or hung, for one second with the gaff poised, so. Then with a swift movement I——

(*Standing unsteadily on the settee he swings up the poker as the door opens and* MILDRED *in her dressing-gown stands in the doorway.* MIRANDA, *sitting on the floor, hidden from her by the sofa, creeps round the end, upstage.* DENYS *sits on the arm of chair below the fire.*)

MILDRED (*to* C.). Adrian! What *are* you doing? (*He is balancing on the settee.*) Do your exercises at home, if you must do them.

ADRIAN. Yes—I—I was just showing Denys——

MILDRED (*crossing to* ADRIAN *below the table*). Well, really I'm afraid you must show him some other time. You woke me up. I heard voices and wondered—— Good gracious, man, you're soaking !

ARTHUR. He—er—fell in the river.

ADRIAN. Yes. I just—fell in. (*He gets off the settee, replacing the poker.*)

MILDRED (*turning to* ARTHUR *and feeling the front of his coat*). And did you fall in, too ?

ARTHUR. No, but of course I had to fish him out of the mess he'd got himself into. I'm quite dry at the back.

MILDRED. I never heard of anything so ridiculous as fishing in the dark. You've never done it before.

ARTHUR. And something tells me we won't do it again.

MILDRED. I should think not, indeed. Adrian (*crossing* R. *a few steps*) go home and get those wet things off and have a hot bath. Why didn't you go straight home, you foolish fellow ?

ADRIAN (*below the settee*). I suppose because nobody would care if I died of pleurisy to-morrow, so it doesn't matter.

MILDRED. Of course they would. What d'you mean ?

ARTHUR. He's raving. He came back because he wanted to say thank you to me.

MILDRED. He could have said that surely when you pulled him out. You know, there's something very fishy about this.

DENYS. You're telling them !

MILDRED (*pushing* ADRIAN *across her to her* L.). Run a'ong now. Adrian.

(ADRIAN *goes up* L. *of the table to up* C.)

I'm glad you had the sense to sleep indoors to-night, Denys.

DENYS.   So am I.   Except that I'm having rather a disturbed night.

MILDRED (*turning and taking* ADRIAN *up to the garden door*). Really, Adrian, for a great grown man to go and fall into a river . . . you should be ashamed of yourself.

ADRIAN.   I am.

MILDRED.   Well, run along now.   (*Opening the garden door.*) And put some mustard in the bath.

(ADRIAN *goes to the door.*)

ADRIAN (*in the doorway*).   Well—er—good night, everybody, and—er——

ARTHUR.   Now don't bother to thank me again.   It was just an unfortunate slip.

ADRIAN.   It was—and the port was much too good.   Good night.

(*He disappears into the garden.*)

MILDRED (*closing the door*).   Port ?   What does he mean ? (*Coming down* C.)   Arthur, you hadn't been drinking ?

ARTHUR (L.C.).   Certainly not.   He's probably slightly delirious.

MILDRED.   I suppose—it *was* an accident.

ARTHUR (*indignantly*).   D'you think I pushed him in ?

DENYS.   Ah !   That opens up a new field of enquiry.   Did he fall or was he pushed ?

MILDRED.   No, no.   (*Leading* ARTHUR *down* L.)   I mean, I believe he—he had a talk with Mary this afternoon.   You don't think——

ARTHUR (*solemnly*).   No.   I don't think so.   I think it was just a mistake, a false step taken in a moment of mental aberration.

MILDRED.   I do hope so.   (*Turning away up* L.C.)   I'm sure it must have been.   Arthur, come along.   You know how easily you catch cold.   Drink that quickly and your bath'll be ready— I hope.   (*Crossing to the door.*)   Be quick now, and be quiet, I've got some aspirins upstairs.

(*She goes out* L.)

MIRANDA (*in a hoarse whisper—reappearing*).   Don't you think Mr. Barasford should go on the films ?

(*The garden door opens with a crack and* ADRIAN'S *head comes round it.*)

ADRIAN.   Arthur, about Pecker !   How much ready money have you ?

ARTHUR (*moving up* C.). I don't know. Why?

ADRIAN (*coming in to* L. *of the bay*). Someone may have to bail him out to-morrow.

ARTHUR (*up to* R. *of* ADRIAN). I'd thought of that. Denys can do it. After all, Sam's our gardener—it would look quite natural. We'll scout round in the morning to find out if they've got him.

ADRIAN. You'd better take this. (*Taking out some notes.*) It's all I've got on me. It'll be all right when it's dry. I haven't much more at home. I meant to go to the Bank yesterday.

ARTHUR (*taking the notes*). I haven't got a lot, but enough with this, I think.

DENYS. They may not have got him.

ADRIAN. We'll give him the stake money, eh, Arthur?

ARTHUR. And pay his fine, of course, if he has been caught. Good night.

ADRIAN. It's no good wishing me that. I shan't sleep a wink. (*He sneezes.*) Oh dear!

(*He disappears through the garden door.*)

ARTHUR (*coming down* L.C.). Come on, Miranda, up you go. We don't want you to get a wigging, too.

MIRANDA (*crossing to* ARTHUR *and kissing him*). Thank you for a wonderful night.

ARTHUR. You'd no right to be there. Good night.

(*He exits* L. DENYS *has moved to below the table.* MIRANDA *comes down* L. *of the table, to him.*)

MIRANDA. Good night, and thank you, too.

DENYS. Good night. (*Very gently.*) Sleep well.

(MIRANDA *looks up at him for a second, then, smiling shakily, she rises on tiptoe, kisses his cheek and darts out* L. DENYS *stands quite still, in front of the table* C., *facing* L.)

CURTAIN.

ACT III

SCENE.—*The same as Acts I and II.* *About 6 p.m. on Sunday evening.*

When the CURTAIN *rises* BELLA, *with* MIRANDA, *is clearing away the remains of the tea-things.* ARTHUR, *on the settee, is reading the "Sunday Times."* DENYS *is seated, sketching in the chair below the fire.* MILDRED *enters with a saucer in one hand and a pile of old books under the other arm. She closes the door behind her and crosses below the table to the fire.*)

MILDRED (*holding out the saucer to* ARTHUR). Arthur, is that stiff or isn't it?

ARTHUR (*solemnly, examining the saucer*). I'd say it was stiff.

MILDRED. And yet nine two-pound pots of the stuff are still running all over the place. (*Sitting on the chair above the fire.*) We may have to take it back with us in the car and boil it all over again.

ARTHUR. In the car? God forbid!

MILDRED. I hope He will. (*She starts going through the top book of the pile which she has dumped down beside her.*)

BELLA (*to* MIRANDA). Old-fashioned stoves is all alike—temperamental. (*She is mostly* L. *of the table.*) Not but what I prefer this oven to the new-fangled affair in the flat. I like a good clean out and a bit of nice black-leadin'. Will you have the jam spoon?

MIRANDA (*taking it*). Thank you.

BELLA. However, there it is and you can't make a better of it.

MIRANDA. And you have the Movies in town.

BELLA. Yes, there's that, and I must say I enjoy them. Did you see that fellow what's-his-name in that thing about the hotel? Tch! What was it called again? You know, that funny little fellow with the whiskers?

MIRANDA. I'm not sure that I do.

BELLA (*brushing up crumbs*). It was a scream! You see, there was these two fellows in love with this girl and there was a robbery going on, so he got himself up as a charwoman and in he went. And this fellow that was in love with the girl—at least, he wasn't really, it was the other fellow that was——

(ARTHUR *lowers his paper and listens.*)

He was clingin' on to the side of the bus followin' the other that had come out by then, and 'e says: "Excuse me, you've dropped something"—and the way 'e said it! Eh, I made a fool of meself larffin'.

67

(MILDRED *stops reading and listens.*)

Oh yes, but before this, there was a woman and a daughter who was really the heirs to all this money, you see, though they didn't know it—would you mind takin' the other end of the cloth ? Thanks—well, you see, these two, not knowin' of course, was helpin' this fellow Simpson to rob them. Not to muddle you, Simpson was the one that wasn't in love with the girl, only pretendin' to be. And they kept goin' round and round this lake until the young fellow, the fair one, turned out to be a detective and got them just when they thought they was clear away. And, mind you, I did too. And at the end all this woman with the daughter says is : " Well, I *said* his eyes was set too close." Eh, she was a yell.

(MIRANDA *moves to the door to open it for* BELLA.)

You ought to see it. I know what it was called—" Up the Pole."

(*She exits through the door* L., *with the tray. They all look at each other.*)

MILDRED. I think we must see " Up the Pole " after that.
ARTHUR. It'll be spoilt for us now we know the plot.
DENYS. It was kind of her not to want to muddle us.
MIRANDA. I suppose it was all quite clear to her.
DENYS (*rising*). Well—I'd better be thinking of packing and collecting the car. (*He leaves the sketch book on the chair.*)
MILDRED. But why, when we'll all be going in half an hour ?
DENYS. I've got to see Perry to-night. I rang up this afternoon and he'll be back about seven.
MILDRED. But why to-night ?
DENYS (*crossing* L., *below the table*). Because when I left him on Friday I'd practically said I was going with him to America, so the sooner he hears I'm not, the better. (*He reaches the door.*)
MIRANDA (L.C.). Denys !
MILDRED. You're not going ?
DENYS (*turning in the* L. *doorway*). No.
MIRANDA. I'll take your tent down for you.
DENYS. Can you ?
MIRANDA (*turning up to the bay*). Of course I can.

(*She exits into the garden.*)

DENYS. Then thanks very much.

(*He exits* L.)

MILDRED (*looking at* ARTHUR). Is Miranda responsible ?
ARTHUR. Or was it last night's cocktails ?
MILDRED. If it were I wish I knew the recipe.
ARTHUR. Where's Mary got to ?

MILDRED. She's gone over to her garden to pick some Michaelmas daisies for us to take home in the car.

(ARTHUR *groans, but* MILDRED *takes no notice.*)

Arthur dear, (*rising*) just glance through these and make sure they're all suitable for Mr. Mallow's Boys' Club. (*She hands him the pile of books.*) I've been promising him some for ages. I wish I was sure about that jam—p'raps it didn't boil hard enough——

(ARTHUR *is looking through one of the books.* MILDRED *goes to the window above the fire.*)

—simmer is such an elastic word.

ARTHUR. Who's Reginald Nightingale ?

MILDRED. Never heard of him. Why ?

ARTHUR. This book was apparently given him by one, " Alice," in nineteen-twenty-four.

MILDRED. Dear me ! It's curious how, in cottages, one always accumulates books belonging to people one's never heard of. (*She moves away from the window, crossing* L.)

ARTHUR. Very. (*Looking at another.*) This one's Adrian's.

MILDRED. He won't want it now. Just dip now, Arthur, don't get absorbed. Oh ! (*Stopping in the doorway.*) Arthur, did you take round the organ money ?

ARTHUR (*jumping up and turning above the settee to* C.). My God !—I mean,—oh yes, at least—no, as a matter of fact, I didn't.

MILDRED. Arthur, really ! Now they'll call before we can get away and I know what'll happen. You'll disappear and I'll have to hear all about the old lady's operation by myself. (*Crossing to him.*) Give me the money and I'll send Miranda round with it now.

ARTHUR. But—er——

MILDRED. But what ? (*Holding out her hand.*) Come along —the sooner it's done the better.

ARTHUR. I—I can't give you the money.

MILDRED. Why not ?

ARTHUR. I haven't got it.

MILDRED. Haven't got it ? Then what have you done with it ?

ARTHUR. Well, I—I lent it to Adrian.

MILDRED. But why did Adrian want money ?

ARTHUR. Well, I think I know, but I'd rather not say.

MILDRED. But you'd no right to lend Adrian the organ fund money—besides, you had it last night.

ARTHUR. He only borrowed it last night.

MILDRED. How much ?

ARTHUR. Three pounds ten.

MILDRED. But it's ridiculous. To-day's Sunday. What on earth could Adrian have wanted to buy with three pounds ten on a Sunday ?

ARTHUR. Perhaps—er——

(ADRIAN *enters from the garden, and comes above the table down* C., *between them.*)

ADRIAN. Good afternoon—good evening, really, I suppose.

MILDRED. Good evening, Adrian, I'm very angry with you.

ADRIAN. With me ? Oh dear, oh dear, you've heard, then ?

MILDRED. I have, and what I really want to know is why you wanted it ?

ADRIAN. I didn't want it at all, that wasn't the point. I just thought it would be easy money—at the time.

MILDRED. Did you !

ADRIAN. You see, it was the dinner——

ARTHUR (*frowning at him*). Adrian, be honest. Admit you wanted the money to settle a bet.

ADRIAN (*lost, but supporting* ARTHUR). Oh ! Did I ?

MILDRED. Surely you know whether you did or not ?

ADRIAN (*rising to the occasion*). Yes, of course I did. I thought it would be easy money, but it wasn't, so I had to settle, you see.

MILDRED. You may as well know you settled it with quite a large part of the church's automatic bellows and I don't approve at all.

ARTHUR. It was partly my fault. (*He breaks a little up* R.)

MILDRED. It was. You had no right to lend it.

(ADRIAN *sneezes.*)

Oh, my dear man, you have caught a cold.

ADRIAN. No, no, it's nothing.

MILDRED. Sit down by the fire ; (*turning away to* L.) I'll come and dose you in a minute.

(*She goes out, shutting the door.* ADRIAN *looks at the door, then turns to* ARTHUR.)

ADRIAN. What was all that ?

ARTHUR. I had to say I'd lent you the money that Denys gave to Pecker this morning. I'd forgotten about those damned bellows.

ADRIAN. I *see.* (*Moving across to the fireplace.*) I say, I was very upset when I heard Pecker had been caught. Poor man, and it was all our fault. Arthur, I do apologize for not coming round earlier. I fell asleep about six and slept the whole day. Have you seen Pecker ?

ARTHUR (*moving down towards him*). No, but Denys bailed him out this morning. (*He sits on the settee.*)

ADRIAN. We ought to see him, don't you think ? I feel so guilty—in one way. In another, I admit I feel a kind of frightful pride in my own prowess. An episode like last night's does make you feel—younger, though of course ashamed at the same time. (*He sneezes.*)

ARTHUR. In spite of a cold, you seem to be feeling better than you did last night.

ADRIAN. Well, it was an adventure—something new. (*He sits above the fireplace.*) And it hasn't really hurt anyone. I mean, Pecker's reputation was by no means flawless before.

ARTHUR. He isn't worrying. He told Denys it would have been worth it if he'd had to pay his fine himself.

ADRIAN. I wonder what he meant by that.

ARTHUR (*smiling*). I don't.

ADRIAN. It's a curious situation—I hope he doesn't slip up on any of his answers. It'll be an anxious time for me.

ARTHUR. We'll have him well primed beforehand.

ADRIAN. I don't like that expression. It's—well . . . I must warn you, Arthur, I shall fine us very heavily.

ARTHUR. Conscience money.

ADRIAN. Yes. And I shall roundly denounce poaching in no uncertain terms. (*Rising.*) What about popping round to Pecker's ? It won't take us a second and I'd like to be here when . . .

(MARCIA *enters from the garden.*)

MARCIA. I can't bear any more—I really can *not* !

ARTHUR (*turning*). Now what's wrong ?

(ADRIAN *moves down below the fire.*)

MARCIA (*above the table, slightly* L. *of* C.). Jim's mending the fence and he's given himself a bogey for each nail—so many strokes to drive it home. He was three under fours a moment ago, but (*desperately*) now something's gone wrong with his swing or his hammer and he's taken six for the last two !

ARTHUR (*soothingly*). Cheer up. (*He rises.*) We'll be going home soon.

MARCIA. He'll be hammering all night at home if he doesn't get it right. D'you think I could send for something to put in his tea ?

ADRIAN. In his tea ?

MARCIA. You can get stuff for smokers and drug addicts—there ought to be something for golf fiends.

(JIM *enters, looking worried.*)

JIM (*to above the table* R. *of* C.). I say, sir, have you such a thing as one of those wooden affairs you mash potatoes with ?

ARTHUR. I don't know——

MARCIA. I'll go and see. (*Moving away* L.) In fact, I'll go and borrow one if it'll do any good.

JIM (*slightly surprised*). Thank you, darling.

(MARCIA *exits* L.)

This hammer . . . (*using it on the air*) something wrong with the shank. I don't know—not whippy enough——

(MILDRED *enters* L.)

MILDRED (*to* C.). Arthur, we can't move the damper and it isn't safe to leave it heating the water. Will you come and see what you can do with it ?

ARTHUR (*sighing, and crossing* L. *below the table*). I'm a sort of plumber's mate in this house.

(*He exits* L.)

MILDRED (*at the door*). And don't dare—any of you—to put any more coal on that fire. I want it to go out, and look at it— thoroughly contrary. You'll have to hurry with the fence, Jim.

JIM (*gloomily*). It's nearly finished. Marcia's bringing me another hammer.

MILDRED. Good. Sorry to leave you like this, Adrian. Entertain him, Jim.

(*She exits* L. ADRIAN *is at the fire.* JIM *looks at him, then takes a pocket book containing snapshots from his coat which hangs on the back of a chair.*)

JIM. Er won't you sit down, sir ? (*He indicates the chair* R. *of the table.*)

(ADRIAN *gives* JIM *a slightly surprised look, then moves to* R. *of the table and sits.*)

ADRIAN (*as he crosses*). Well, I was going out in a minute. . . . (*He sits.*)

(JIM *sits* C., *above the table, and opens the pocket book.*)

JIM. Are you interested in photography at all, sir ?

ADRIAN. Oh—yes——

JIM. It's my little hobby—just taken it up, really. I've got some rather interesting ones (*jocularly*) of my son and heir here. (*Handing him one.*)

ADRIAN. Oh—thank you——

JIM. That's under-exposed a bit, but the light wasn't too good. He's asleep in his pram.

ADRIAN. I see.

JIM. And here he is playing with the dog. I seem to have cut off the top of his head. He's devoted to the dog, you know— in fact he's a real animal lover. You should hear him when the cows are coming in. " Gid up ! " he says. He can imitate anything.

ADRIAN. Remarkable.

JIM. It is, you know. Dash it all, I mean, he's only three. The other day he made us laugh. I came down the stairs and he was sitting in his chair, and he suddenly said " Richard's going to say damn "—and by Jove, he did. You never know what he'll be up to next.

(MARCIA *enters* L., *unobserved, with a potato masher.*)

That's him on my knee outside our front door.

ADRIAN. Was it taken at night ?

JIM. No-o. Over-exposed a bit, perhaps.

MARCIA. Put them away, Jim.

JIM (*thoroughly annoyed*). You know, you're a most unnatural mother !

MARCIA. My dear Jim, he's a very ordinary child of three——

JIM. But that's just what he isn't. If he was, I wouldn't be so interested in him.

MARCIA. Oh Jim, you idiot, shut up !

JIM (*jumping up*). Marcia !

ADRIAN (*rising*). I say—er—I think I'll have a look round the garden . . .

(ADRIAN *goes out into the garden hastily.*)

JIM. I wish you wouldn't say things like that. It's—it's—well, it's very rude, and——

MARCIA (*crossing* R. *below the table*). But you're such a fathead.

JIM (*following her down to* L. *of the settee*). Anyone would think you didn't care for him. They would, really——

MARCIA (*turning below the settee*). How dare you say such a thing when you know it isn't true ?

JIM. According to you he's always plain, dull, and——

MARCIA. What a lie ! He's sweet, and very good-looking, *and* interesting !

JIM. But——

MARCIA. But it's no good telling people so, they've got to find out for themselves. No child's ordinary to its parents, but you can pretend it is—if you've got any sense—which you apparently haven't. You're infuriating, Jim. (*She raises the potato masher.*) A hundred times a day I *long* to——

JIM (*suddenly assuming the offensive*). Don't *you* wave that thing at me !

MARCIA. I'll wave it where I like—I'll *use* it where I like and the more strokes I take the better !——

JIM (*seizing her arm*). Give that to me ! (*He snatches it from her and sits her suddenly and firmly on the arm of the settee.*) Now ! Listen to me.

MARCIA. I will not. (*She smacks her hand down on the back of the settee.*)

JIM (*rapping her smartly over the knuckles with the potato masher*). Oh yes, you will.

MARCIA (*standing, and backing a pace*). Jim!——

JIM. Do I drink?

MARCIA (*nursing her hand*). I never thought so—until now.

JIM. I don't. You know I don't. Do I run after other women?

MARCIA. No.

JIM. Very well, then, why do you——?

MARCIA. I sometimes wish you did. It might make things more interesting.

(*A short pause.*)

JIM. D'you mean that?

MARCIA. Well, it couldn't be——

JIM (*loudly*). *Do you mean that?*

MARCIA (*louder still*). *Yes!*

JIM. Right! It may interest you to know that Rowena Whatever-her-name-is gave me her telephone number and asked me to ring her up some time when I was in town. I shall ring her to-morrow. (*He turns up* L. *of the table.*)

MARCIA (*to below the* R. *end of the table*). Jim, don't be so silly!

JIM (*facing* MARCIA). You spend your life criticizing me, now you can have something to criticize. (*He goes up into the bay and turns to her.*) D'you know what she said to me?

MARCIA. No, and I don't want to.

JIM. She said that deep down in my eyes there were hidden fires.

MARCIA (*turning away* R. *to the fire*). She's a fool.

JIM. I thought so at the time, but now I'm not so sure she isn't right. Anyway, it might be interesting to find out.

(*He sweeps out, passing* ADRIAN *and* MARY *entering from the garden.* MARY'S *arms are full of flowers and Michaelmas daisies.* MARCIA *has moved up to the top end of the settee.*)

MARY. Jim seems in a hurry. Where's the fire?

MARCIA (*viciously*). In his eyes. Didn't you notice?

ADRIAN (*on the rostrum,* L. *of* MARY). I beg your pardon?

MARCIA. Don't bother.

(*She turns away and looks out of the window above the fire.* MARY *comes down* R.C. *a little.* ARTHUR *enters* L.)

ARTHUR (*to* L.C.). The damper is in, the jam is showing faint signs of setting, and the plumbing seems safe for the moment—so come along, Adrian, let's get our visit over.

ADRIAN. But I don't—oh yes, of course, we have to call on Pecker. Forgive me. We shan't be long. (*He turns to the garden door.*)

ARTHUR (*following*). Five minutes.

(*They exit by the garden door.*)

MARY (*regarding* MARCIA'S *back*). It may be a fine day, but I sense electricity in the atmosphere. (*A short pause.*) Or am I imagining things ?

MARCIA (*turning, furiously*). Jim says I'm always criticizing him. I'm not, am I ?

MARY (*cheerfully*). Yes, my dear, you are.

MARCIA. Aunt Mary !

MARY. In fact, if you're not very careful you're going to turn into a nagging wife.

MARCIA (*staggered*). Nagging ? Me ?

MARY. Oh, you think you're doing it in Jim's interests, I know. You're so afraid he's boring people.

MARCIA. But he *is*. I know he is.

MARY (*crossing to sit in the chair* L., *putting the flowers up* L. *on her way*). Nonsense, and it's his affair if he is—not yours. He's a very delightful and very genuine person, you know. (*She sits.*)

MARCIA (R.C.). Others apparently think that as well as you. (*To above the* L. *end of the table.*) That wretched woman Denys brought here's been putting ideas into his head.

MARY. Well, you have only yourself to blame. You should have got in first.

MARCIA (*scornfully*). Can you imagine telling your husband there were hidden fires deep down in his eyes ?

MARY. Easily. Why not ? (*Becoming roused.*) I've never been able to understand why a man should cease to be worth flirting with once you've married him.

MARCIA. But——

MARY. Go along. Stop telling him what he's doing wrong and tell him what he does right for a change. You've got a trump card Rowena can't touch.

MARCIA. What ?

MARY. Richard.

MARCIA (*groaning*). Oh heavens ! (*Turning a little to* C.) I suppose I ought to learn to play golf, too ?

MARY. I would, if I were you.

MARCIA. Yes, but . . . (*With a heavy sigh.*) Oh dear, I suppose you're right. (*She moves to* L. *of the upper end of the settee.*)

MARY. I know I am.

(MILDRED *enters, with a Japanese basket which she starts to pack on the table* C.)

MILDRED. Thank goodness, it's beginning to go gluey round
the sides at last. Have you packed, Marcia ?

MARCIA. Yes.

MILDRED. Good. Arthur can start packing the car.

MARCIA (*moving to the garden door, picking up* JIM'S *coat from
the chair on her way*). You know, Aunt Mary, you must have a
very nice nature. (*Turning in the bay.*) All the same I swear
you've never had to live with someone who would always have
gone round in seventy-nine if he hadn't had a seven at the
fourteenth.

(*She exits to the garden.*)

MILDRED (*smiling*). Silly girl. (*Seeing* MARY'S *flowers she
goes to them.*) Mary, my dear, how lovely—and what a lot !
(*To* L.C.) Where are Arthur and Adrian ?

MARY. Gone to call on Mr. Pecker, I believe.

MILDRED. I meant to give Adrian some quinine.

MARY. I thought he seemed to have a cold.

MILDRED. D'you wonder ? (*She crosses to the dresser with
the basket.*) Falling into the river in the middle of the night.
(*She takes the gingerbread from the tin in the dresser and packs it
into the basket.*)

MARY (*rising*). What d'you mean ? (*To* R. *of* MILDRED.)
Did Adrian fall into the river ? How did he do it ?

MILDRED. I don't know. Well—forgive me, Mary—but I
knew he was going to speak to you yesterday, and when I found
him soaked to the skin he said something about no one caring
if he died and I thought for a moment that because you'd refused
him, he might have—but of course he didn't, I'm quite sure——
(*She hands* MARY *the empty cake tin, indicates that she should
return it to the dresser and crosses back to the table* C.)

MARY. Mildred, what *are* you talking about ? (*Putting the
tin away.*) What d'you mean by " refused him " ? (*To the
armchair* L.) He offered to sell me his house, and I refused that,
I admit, but he hardly threw himself into the river on that
account.

MILDRED. Sell you his house ?

MARY. He stressed the fact that it had two bathrooms and
that mine had none.

MILDRED. Oh, my goodness ! What has the lunatic done
now ?

MARY. D'you mean—— (*She crosses to* L. *of the table.*) Oh,
Mildred, you're dreaming !

MILDRED. I'm not. He told me himself—— (*Suddenly
sitting* C., *above the table.*) I'm going to tell you, because it's
obvious he never will. He's been nursing a hopeless passion for
you for months, and yesterday I urged him to tell you about it.

MARY. Did you ?

MILDRED. Oh dear !—I remember saying his house was more comfortable than yours. He must have been using it as a—sort of bait.

MARY (*laughing suddenly*). Poor Adrian. But I still don't know why he fell into the river in the middle of the night.

MILDRED. Well, he and Arthur were fishing, and——

MARY. In the middle of the night ?

MILDRED. You know what these fishermen are.

(MARY *shakes her head and crosses thoughtfully below the table, to the fire.*)

MARY. I hear your guest departed rather suddenly.

MILDRED. Don't ! I'm so ashamed, I feel that I've failed as a hostess. Really, Denys is stupid. We weren't at all what the poor girl was expecting.

MARY. Is Miranda back in favour ?

MILDRED. Very much so—I think.

MARY. It was playing into Miranda's hands for them to meet here. She looks very nice in a mackintosh.

MILDRED. Now, Mary ! That's peeping into Volume Two. (*Rising.*) I'm going to slip across to Doris Debrett's for the eggs. Come with me.

(*She turns up* C. MARY *follows her up.* MIRANDA *enters by the garden door with a tent rolled up.*)

MIRANDA. I've taken down Denys's tent for him.

MILDRED. How very nice of you.

MIRANDA. D'you know where the straps are ?

MILDRED. In the hall, I think.

(MILDRED *and* MARY *exit into the garden.* MIRANDA *dumps the tent by the banisters and tries to roll it up tighter.* BELLA *enters carrying a parcel.*)

BELLA. Where's the mistress ?

MIRANDA (*indicating the garden*). Just gone out.

BELLA (*going up to the bay*). I'd better wait, then. (*Checking, up* C.) Sam Pecker brought this, but I'd give it to the mistress when she was alone. P'raps you'd do it for me ? I've got enough on me 'ands. Don't you let anyone see it. (*She moves down and gives the parcel to* MIRANDA.)

MIRANDA (*airily, crossing up* R.). Mr. Pecker didn't happen to mention where he spent last night, did he ? (*She puts the parcel on the ground, behind the settee, covering it with a cushion.*)

BELLA (*sniffing*). He did not, and I'm sure I'm not interested. Last week he told me he was goin' to the concert, and when I got there, there was no sign of 'im. You know, there's some fellers seem to think you're like a ripe cherry on a tree, just waitin' to drop off into their mouths when they say the word. Well, 'e'll learn different from me. " I'm like time and tide," I says to 'im, " I wait for no man."

(ADRIAN *enters from the window.*)

Good evenin', sir. I must get on with me cleaning up.

(*She exits* L.)

MIRANDA (L. *of the settee*). Hello! How are you feeling to-day ?

ADRIAN (L.C.). Sh !

MIRANDA. That's a very harmless question.

ADRIAN. I suppose it is, but nothing seems harmless to-day. (*He crosses down to the chair below the fire.*) We've just called at Pecker's cottage, but he was out.

MIRANDA. He called here a few minutes ago.

ADRIAN. That's very vexing.

(MILDRED *appears with* MARY *at the garden door.* MILDRED *moves down, above the table.*)

MILDRED. I must have a look at my jam. Miranda, put some newspaper round these, will you ? (*Handing her some eggs.*) We don't want them broken. You'll find some in the boot cupboard.

(MIRANDA *moves* L. MILDRED *follows.*)

I'll come with you. (*To* MARY, *who begins to follow.*) No, no, dear, you stay here. Come on, Miranda.

(MILDRED *and* MIRANDA *exit* L.)

MARY (*after a glance at* ADRIAN, *sitting in the armchair above the fire*). What's this I hear about you falling into the river last night ?

ADRIAN (*jumping*). Who told you ?

MARY. Mildred. Why ? Didn't you want me to know ?

ADRIAN. Yes, of course, but it was such a foolish thing to do. Ridiculous, really——

MARY. Do you often fish in inky blackness ?

ADRIAN. No, but you see it makes the light more effective.

MARY. Light ?.

ADRIAN. Did I say " light " ? Ha, ha ! I meant to say " line." Would you mind if we changed the subject ? You know how unpleasant it is to be reminded of one's foolish actions.

MARY. Of course not. What shall we talk about ?

ADRIAN. Well now, let me see. (*Rising and sitting on the settee.*)

(*There is a pause.*)

MARY. Adrian !

ADRIAN. Yes ?

MARY. I've been wondering—whether I misunderstood something you said to me yesterday.

ADRIAN. Something I said ? (*Moving nearer her.*)

MARY. Yes. It suddenly occurred to me that perhaps I had.

ADRIAN. But yesterday I said—I asked—when we were in here, d'you mean ?

MARY. Yes.

ADRIAN. But—but—(*miserably*) I wish I knew for certain what you meant.

MARY. Well, when you were talking about your house——

ADRIAN (*eagerly*). Yes ?

MARY. You weren't trying to sell it to me ?

ADRIAN. Sell it ? Good heavens, no !

MARY. I thought you were. I'm so sorry.

ADRIAN. No, no, I was just—feeling my way, as it were. I thought—— (*Suddenly rising from the settee.*) Mary, I've changed since yesterday. I'm not going to beat about the bush any longer. I——

MARY (*hastily, as* ARTHUR'S *voice is heard*). No, wait a minute—not here, Adrian. Come to dinner to-morrow.

ADRIAN. No ! I might have changed back again by then.

(ARTHUR *enters through the garden door.*)

ARTHUR. I say, Adrian . . .

ADRIAN (*turning*). Go away, Arthur, I'm talking to Mary.

ARTHUR (*staggered*). But——

ADRIAN. Go away ! (*Very loudly.*)

MARY. Adrian——

ARTHUR. I'm damned if I will.

ADRIAN. Then we will. Come along, Mary, we'll go into the garden. (*Pulling her up.*)

MARY (*standing below the armchair above the fire*). No, no !

ARTHUR. Look here, it's all right. I'll go. (*Breaking* L.) I didn't understand——

MARY (*firmly*). Arthur, we're none of us going.

(ARTHUR *checks, up* L.C.)

Adrian, you shall escort me home to-night, and in the meantime you *must* continue to beat about the bush a little longer. And don't worry, my dear, it's quite all right.

ADRIAN (*to her*). Oh, Mary—oh, dear !——

ARTHUR. I say, I feel most embarrassed——

ADRIAN. And so you should.

(BELLA *enters* L. *and proceeds to search the drawers of the dresser.*)

BELLA. Excuse me. (*Going to the dresser* L.)

ARTHUR. Go for your tour of the garden——

MARY. We might all go out there, mightn't we ? It's too fine to be indoors.

ARTHUR. Well, but——

MARY. Arthur, don't be a fool ! I'm twice as embarrassed as you are.

ARTHUR. Very well then. (*Crossing up to the bay.*) Come along then.

(*He exits into the garden.*)

ADRIAN. Mary, do you really mean what I think you do ?

MARY. I'll tell you to-night. (*Holding out her hand to him.*) Come along.

ADRIAN. Oh, Mary. (*He is about to kiss her hand, but sees* BELLA.)

(*They go out, joining* ARTHUR *in the garden.* MILDRED *enters* L.)

MILDRED (*to* BELLA). Have you found them ? (*She crosses to* C.)

BELLA (*at the dresser*). It would be a lie to say that I have. And yet I'd swear I put them in here after we tied down the raspberry.

(MIRANDA *enters with straps.*)

Half a minute !—here they are ! (*She takes out some jam covers.*)

MILDRED. Thank goodness ! Miranda, if you want a job, would you like to write the jam-covers for me ?

MIRANDA (*putting the straps round the tent,* R.C.). I will in a minute.

MILDRED. Thank you, dear. My pen's on the mantelpiece. (*Turning up* C.) I'm going to cut some cabbages.

(*She goes out into the garden.*)

BELLA (*putting some jam-covers on the table*). Bramble, or Blackberry, whichever you like. We'll need ten two-pound. And would you mind printin' them ? Miss Marcia did some one year and you couldn't tell the rhubarb-and-ginger from red-currant-and-rasp.

(*She goes out* L.)

ARTHUR (*leaning in through the window*). Is that the " Sunday Times," Miranda ?

MIRANDA (*picking it up from the settee*). Yes. (*She takes it up and hands it to him.*)

ARTHUR. Thanks.

MIRANDA. Have you got a pencil ?

ARTHUR. Yes, thank you.

(MIRANDA *gets the pen from the mantelpiece and sits down at the table with the jam-covers.* DENYS *enters* L. *with his suitcase which he puts down* L.C.)

DENYS (*looking at the tent*). Hello! Did you do that?
MIRANDA. I did. It was quite dry.
DENYS. Thank you very much.
MIRANDA. I couldn't pull the straps quite tight enough.
DENYS. It'll do, I think. (*He takes it out and dumps it outside* L., *and then re-enters, humming.*)
MIRANDA. Denys, why aren't you going to America?
DENYS. Because I don't want to. Now, for God's sake, don't start a dissertation on why you think I *ought*.
MIRANDA. I wasn't going to. I wanted to know whether it was because you wanted to work, or just because—you'd quarrelled with Rowena?
DENYS. A bit of both, probably. (*He moves up to the windows and round the room, collecting book, sketch book, slippers, pipe, etc., throughout the following speeches.*)
MIRANDA (*after a pause, writing hard, abruptly*). Sorry I was so dotty last night.
DENYS. That's all right.
MIRANDA. I mean about weeping. I don't weep much as a rule.
DENYS. I'll have my dressing-gown pressed and send the bill in to you.
MIRANDA. All right. (*A pause.*) Are you very unhappy about her?
DENYS. My heart is breaking, but I'm concealing it under a brave show of nonchalance.
MIRANDA. No, but are you—really?
DENYS. Don't you think I am?
MIRANDA. I mean, unhappy?
DENYS. Not in the least. I like her—she amuses me. We haven't really quarrelled, you know.
MIRANDA. I'm so glad.

(DENYS *looks at her standing* R. *of the table.*)

DENYS. I thought you would be. You did all you could to bring us together.
MIRANDA. Yes, I did my best.
DENYS. Now, what else belongs to me? (*He takes a book from the settee, crosses* L.C., *and opens his suitcase.*) When do you go to Paris?
MIRANDA. Next month, for two years. There'll be no one to—be a nuisance to you then.
DENYS. No. There won't be.
MIRANDA. You'll probably marry some frightful creature.

(DENYS *looks round.*)

Oh, sorry ! I mean—well—honestly, I'm not being catty, but you don't always choose awfully wisely, do you ? (*Hastily.*) I don't mean Rowena, of course—I mean—well——

DENYS. Let it pass, let it pass.

MIRANDA. Oh, heavens, I've written rhubarb and ginger.

DENYS. Serves you right. (*A pause. Lightly ; packing his case.*) I shall be over in Paris in November.

(MIRANDA *stops writing and sits very still.* DENYS *stands.*)

Will you dine with me ? Or we might go somewhere for the day —if they'll let you ?

MIRANDA (*tensely*). They'll let me.

DENYS. Good. (*Crossing to her* L., *above the table.*) Then I can tell you all about my latest and you can advise me.

MIRANDA. That'll be—a very good idea. (*Looking up at him.*)

DENYS (*looking down at her affectionately*). You are just a baby, aren't you ?

MIRANDA. I shall grow up very quickly in Paris.

DENYS. Not too quickly. If I'm losing my job, it'll take a long time to make up for it.

MIRANDA. Two years ?

DENYS. Perhaps.

MIRANDA. Try to make it two years, if you can.

DENYS. You never know. (*Up to the bay.*) Good-bye, everybody !

(*General good-byes, from outside.* MILDRED *appears at the window.*)

MILDRED (*outside*). Are you off ? Good-bye, dear, and do drive carefully.

DENYS (*solemnly*). I shall never go above ten miles an hour the entire way, I swear it.

MILDRED. Tell Nora we'll be in about eight for supper.

DENYS. I'll tell her, good-bye. (*He leans out to kiss her.*)

MILDRED. Good-bye, dear. Arthur, dear, do get the car out.

(DENYS *comes down above and* L. *of the table.*)

DENYS (*to* MIRANDA). Good-bye—and be good.

MIRANDA. Good-bye.

DENYS. You've missed the *r* out of " bramble " in that one.

MIRANDA. Have I ?

DENYS (*taking hold of her hand for a minute and shaking it*). See you in November.

(*He picks up his case and goes out* L.)

MILDRED (*re-entering from the garden with some cabbages*). Have you finished those ?

(MIRANDA *nods*.)

—Oh dear, oh dear——

MIRANDA. It's all right—it's just—that he's so sweet!
(*Chokily*.)

MILDRED (*putting her arms round her, from behind*). Yes, well,
he can be when he likes. (*A pause.*) Why isn't he going to
America ? Did he tell you ?

MIRANDA. Not—quite.

MILDRED. Strange . . .   (*Crossing to* R.C.) If you've
finished those will you give them to Bella ? (*Looking at the
parcel by the settee.*) What's that ?

MIRANDA (*rising*). It's a parcel Sam Pecker brought for you.
You can have it now—it had to be given to you when you were
alone.

MILDRED. Dear me ! How very mysterious.

(*She is about to lift it when* DENYS *re-appears* L. *in the doorway.*)

DENYS. Miranda, is your case packed ?

MIRANDA. Yes.

DENYS (*dropping down below the door*). Then come on. I
don't see why I should drive up to town by myself.

MIRANDA. Denys ! (*Jumping up.*) I'm absolutely ready.
Good-bye, Aunt Mildred. Thank you for a *perfect* week-end.
(*Kissing her.*)

MILDRED. But——

(MIRANDA *dashes up to the bay, calls rapid* " good-byes " *through
the window, and flies back into the room.*)

MIRANDA (*seizing the jam-covers*). I'll give these to Bella.
(*She rushes* L.) My hat's in the hall. (*Suddenly stopping as she
gets to the door.*) Isn't life wonderful !

(*She goes out* L. DENYS *and* MILDRED *look at each other.* DENYS
*looks slightly sheepish, but not altogether displeased with himself,
and goes to the door.*)

MILDRED (*doubtfully*). Denys—be careful—don't break her
heart.

DENYS (*turning and smiling at her*). Don't worry, darling.
I'm only afraid she may break mine.

(*He exits* L. MILDRED *picks up the parcel and carries it to the
table.*)

MILDRED (*looking at the contents which are wrapped in newspaper
inside the outer wrapping*). Good heavens ! (*She picks out a note
and reads it ; then stares, thunderstruck in front of her. Calling.*)
Mary ! (*She crosses to the mantelpiece for her spectacles.*)

MARY (*off*). Yes ?

MILDRED (*returning to the table*). Come here, will you—just one minute.

(MARY, *through the window, is seen to rise and cross to the garden door, as* ARTHUR *appears and rejoins* ADRIAN.)

MARY (*calling over her shoulder*). I'm sure " catastrophe " is wrong. (*Entering.*) What is it ? I warn you I know very little about jam.

MILDRED. It isn't jam. Look at that !—(*pointing to the parcel*)—and read that !

MARY (*reading with difficulty*). " Dear Madam, as I know—you—are "—what ?

MILDRED. Fond.

MARY. " As I know you are fond, if—a—bit——"

MILDRED. " *of* a bit "—give it to me. " I am sending the enclosed that some of us got last night and apologize as being your part-time man, for if I appear in court next week as I was caught by the bailiff last night I would not of been but there was reasons considering the parties I was out with and please not to worry as I have a friend at court——"

(MILDRED *and* MARY *look up stage to the windows.*)

" —as you might say and will be all right luckily this afternoon it was still in the branch of the tree where I was quick enough to throw it when they came on us. Hoping you will enjoy what was hard won in the spirit of sport settling a bet between the parties concerned knowing the bailiff was in the concert and expecting the supper afterwards to keep him busy——"—I wish he'd take a breath—" —and assuring you of it never happening again and that I had no hand in it but only to look on hoping your husband is well to-day I am yours obediently Sam Pecker."

(*A pause.*)

MARY (*moving down* L.). Mildred—you don't think——?

MILDRED. That's exactly what I do think. Don't you ?

(JIM *enters with* MARCIA. MILDRED *hastily covers the fish.*)

JIM (*triumphantly*). The fence is finished. Only two strokes apiece for the last four nails.

MARCIA. And *I* did one of them.

JIM (*toying with the potato masher*). Handy little weapon this. Useful for more than one purpose, eh ? No husband should be without it.

(MARCIA *and* JIM *move to the* R. *pillar.* ELLA SPENDER'S *voice is heard.* MILDRED *quickly thrusts the parcel into the armchair* L. *and covers it with a cushion.*)

ELLA (*off*). Mildred !

(*She enters* L.)

Hello, my dear, how are you, Mary ? (*At* L.C.) I've just brought your counterpane back on the way to the choir practice. Wasn't last night *frightful* ?   However, it's over, that's one thing.

(*During the above,* MILDRED *drapes the counterpane over the chair and fish.*)

MARY. I thought it was a most successful concert.

ELLA. Financially—but what about artistically ?

(MARCIA *drops down a li*⁴*le* R.)

MILDRED (*moving a step* R.). Do sit down. (*Edging her to the settee.*)

ELLA. No, no, you're just going, I know. Wasn't Robert's speech dreary ? Still, somebody has to do it. And what do you think ? While Tom Mace was singing and Robert was moving the Vote of Thanks, someone was quietly pinching the only salmon in poor Robert's bit of the river ! We've had the most awful day ! Robert's been going about like somebody bereaved. It wasn't that he ever expected to catch it, but he knew it was there and it gave him hope. It really is heartbreaking.

MILDRED. Dreadful !

.ARTHUR *enters with* ADRIAN *from the garden.* ELLA *goes towards them up stage.*)

ELLA. Arthur, isn't it frightful ! A salmon that Robert's been gloating over for weeks was poached last night.

ADRIAN (*hoarsely*). Robert's ?

ELLA. Yes. Your Mr. Pecker was mixed up in it, by the way, but he swears he only saw the lights and went down to watch. He would say that, of course, but they really do seem to think they were townsfolk for various reasons.

(*She comes down* C. ARTHUR *to* L. *of* C. ADRIAN *sneezes, and envelops himself in a handkerchief.*)

You've got a nasty cold.

ARTHUR. But this—is very upsetting.

ELLA. Upsetting ? Robert aged ten years under my very eyes ! That animal was to him more than just a fish, it was practically a pet.

(ADRIAN *comes down* L.C., *on the* L. *of* ARTHUR.)

MARY (*innocently*). Arthur, you and Adrian were out last night. I suppose you didn't see anyone ?

ARTHUR. No. No, we didn't, did we ?

ADRIAN. No, we didn't.

ARTHUR.   No one at all.

ADRIAN.   No one.

ARTHUR.   Not a soul.

ADRIAN.   No one was about——

MILDRED (L., *by the armchair*).   That's all right.   I think we've gathered now that you didn't see anyone.

ARTHUR (*taking* ELLA *a little* L.).   Won't you sit down ?

ELLA.   No, I—(*looking at the clock*) well, for just two minutes. (*She looks round wondering where to sit.*)

MILDRED.   Sit down, Adrian.   (*Pushing him into the chair* L. *on top of the parcel, which is under the cushion and counterpane.*)

ADRIAN (*struggling*).   But—what's this . . .

MARCIA.   The settee's much more comfortable.

(ELLA *moves to* R. *of the table.*)

ADRIAN (*attempting to remove the bump from his chair*). What's——

MILDRED (*sotto voce*).   Sit still.

(ADRIAN *subsides astonished.*)

ELLA (*sitting* R. *of the table*).   What made it so very annoying was that poor Robert hates taking the chair at things, and if he hadn't had to last night, he'd have been sure to take his evening walk up the river—he always does before his tea at nine-thirty——

ADRIAN.   He'd have been too soon——

ARTHUR (*sitting* C., *above the table—quickly*).   These fellows never start until later than that.

(MILDRED *and* MARY *exchange glances.*)

ELLA.   Of course Tom Mace would have got them easily if he hadn't been at the concert—though as it was he was very lucky to see them at all.   He was just on his way home with Bill and Harry Bates and he saw the light from the Mill Bridge.   He thought he'd just investigate and he caught them practically red-handed.   The annoying thing from my point of view is that he couldn't find the fish.

JIM.   Perhaps they never got one.

ELLA.   Oh, but they did.   He saw it there in the light from their own torch.   It was just that he couldn't find it afterwards.

ADRIAN.   Wasn't it on the bank ?

ELLA.   No, and he said they were all running much too fast to have it with them.

MARY.   Perhaps it flopped itself back into the river and is still there for Robert after all ?

ADRIAN.   Perhaps it is !

ELLA.   D'you think so ?   I'll suggest it to him.   It might comfort him.   Tom Mace recognized Pecker's run, apparently he's chased him before, but he didn't know any of the others.

MILDRED.　How many were there ?

ELLA.　Two men and possibly a boy as well.　They're sure the men were town people because Pecker said he'd never seen them before and Tom Mace said they ran very queerly—like old rams with footrot.

(MARY *and* MILDRED *laugh much too hard.*)

MILDRED (*wiping her eyes*).　Such an amusing expression.

MARY (*feebly*).　Very amusing.

ELLA (*mildly surprised at the success of her remark*).　It's stealing, you know.

MARCIA.　But perhaps they were hungry.

ELLA.　You don't steal *salmon* when you're hungry.　Harry Bates nearly got one of them.　He saw which way he was running and headed him off.　He was waiting behind a bush for him, when suddenly the man turned and did a beautiful swallow dive into the river.

(ADRIAN *gurgles.*)

ARTHUR.　How did Harry see this ?

ELLA.　I don't know, but Harry can't swim, so he had to let him go.

MILDRED.　And what did the other one do ?

ELLA.　Oh !　Bill Bates said the other man ran up the cliff side and hurled great boulders down at him from the top.

ARTHUR.　What ? !

ELLA.　Wasn't it awful ?　You see, they really are dangerous. It might have been manslaughter.　Bill said one only missed him by inches, and the man on the cliff gave a yell of demoniacal laughter

(ARTHUR *snorts and* ADRIAN *giggles.*)

My dear, I must fly !　(*Jumping up and crossing to* MILDRED L.)

MILDRED (*as* ADRIAN *starts to rise*).　Don't get up.　(*She pushes him forcibly down again, meeting* ELLA *at* C.)

ELLA.　Are you coming down next week-end ?

MILDRED.　I hope so.

ELLA.　Couldn't we have a picnic or something really exciting ? I'll take the tea—though it won't be very nice, our big thermos has gone queer.　The children'll be back at school, but I suppose that really makes it pleasanter.　Anyway, I'll pop in on Saturday. (*She crosses* L. *to the door.*)

MILDRED.　Arthur'll be fishing, I expect.

ELLA.　They are trying, aren't they ?　Flies here, and rods there, and a strong (*sniffing*) smell of fish all over the house. Good-bye.

(*She exits* L. ADRIAN *and* ARTHUR *exchange glances and start to rise.*)

MILDRED. Now then! No. Don't get up.

(ARTHUR *and* ADRIAN *subside.*)

We'll have a few explanations, if you please.

ARTHUR. What d'you mean?

MILDRED. Now don't be silly, Arthur. I know who took Robert's salmon. (*She crosses below the table.*)

ADRIAN. But—how?——

MILDRED (*turning up and sitting* R. *of the table*). When people, hitherto apparently quite compos mentis—begin jumping apart when the door opens, and falling into rivers in the middle of the night, and lending people three pounds ten to spend on a Sunday, I begin to wonder why.

ARTHUR. It was a joke——

MARCIA. In very poor taste.

MILDRED. To go dashing about the countryside, doing swallow dives and shrieking with laughter would be undignified at any time, but——

ADRIAN. But I couldn't do a swallow dive to save my life.

ARTHUR. And I couldn't shriek with demoniacal laughter if I tried.

MILDRED. Well, we'll leave that. I suppose Sam Pecker will be given something to soothe his wounded pride?

ARTHUR. Five pounds.

MARY. I suppose you'll impose a fine, Adrian?

ADRIAN. I will indeed, though we'll pay it ourselves, of course.

JIM. I say! That's how you dispense justice, is it?

MILDRED. How much?

ADRIAN. Another five pounds, I expect.

MARY. Ten pounds for a salmon weighing——

ADRIAN (*eagerly*). Twenty pounds at least.

ARTHUR. Not nearly as much.

ADRIAN. It was, Arthur. You didn't feel the weight, I did.

ARTHUR (*rising and crossing to* R. *of* ADRIAN). Now don't call me a liar again, or we shall be back where we started.

ADRIAN (*triumphantly*). You've just admitted you hardly saw it, and yet you insist you know what weight it was.

ARTHUR. I insist I know what weight it *wasn't*.

(BELLA *enters* L., *in a flutter, wearing her hat and coat. She stands on the steps.*)

BELLA. The Vicar's car's just comin' up the hill!

MILDRED. Oh, *no*!

BELLA. It is. I was puttin' the cases in the car.

MARCIA (*jumping up*). Quick! We've gone.

(*Every one jumps up.*)

MILDRED. Going, anyway. (*To* c.) Hurry, Arthur. Get ready! Lock up the back, Bella. That rug's to go to the cleaners. (*Pointing to the rug in front of the fire.*) Roll it up, Jim. Where are the eggs?

(*She darts out* L. BELLA *to the dresser.*)

ARTHUR. My rod! (*He gets it from the corner.*)
MARCIA. Have these books to go? (*Indicating the books on the armchair at the fire.*)
ARTHUR. Yes.

(MARY *puts the basket on the table, and packs it with parcels from* BELLA *and* MILDRED.)

BELLA (*rushing to the table*). The joint's to go in the basket. And this is butter. (*She puts them on the table.*)
MARY. I'll do it.

(MILDRED *darts in.*)

MILDRED. The eggs! Be very careful! And a boiling of potatoes—they'll go in the basket. Scrape the fire apart, some-one, so that it goes out.

(ADRIAN *crosses* R. *and does so.* MILDRED *darts out again* L.)

ARTHUR. Where's my cast case? (*Searching madly—he goes to the dresser.*)

(BELLA *seizes the flowers in the vase on the mantelpiece, pulls them out, tips the water out of the window, puts the vase back, and goes through out to the garden with the flowers.*)

BELLA (*as she exits*). Dustbin.

(MARCIA *goes into the hall* L.)

ADRIAN (*moving to* c.). Can I——?
MARY (*at the table* c.). Fasten this strap.

(JIM *is by the fireplace.* MARCIA *comes back with* ARTHUR'S *and* JIM'S *coats and hats and her own hat.*)

MARCIA (*delivering them round*). Here you are.
ARTHUR (*furiously—still searching down* L. *at the dresser*). I had the damned thing this morning.

(MILDRED *comes in with a bowl and pie-dish which she gives to* MARY.)

MILDRED. Now then—Marcia, the cabbages. Jim, the basket—be careful—I'll bring the eggs. Oh, the rug! Thank you, Jim. The cases are in. Here you are, Arthur. (*She thrusts the Michaelmas daisies and leaves into his arms.*)

Arthur. Oh, lord ! I'll *buy* you some flowers——
Mildred. Don't be silly. Bella will lock up and come out at the front. Oh ! The Boys' Club books !

(Adrian *dashes over and picks them up. The bell rings.*)
Quick !

(Mildred *is at the foot of the steps* c. Arthur *is* r.c. *of the rostrum. The others have already surged towards the garden door.*)

Arthur. Wait ! This time are you *sure* you've forgotten nothing ?
Mildred. Nothing—— (*Stopping suddenly.*) Oh yes, I have.
Marcia ⎫
Arthur ⎭ (*together*).   What ?
Mildred. If you want to know what your fish weighed, you'd better bring it with you—Adrian's been sitting on it !

(*She points to the chair and makes for the garden door, with* Marcia, Mary *and* Jim *looking back over their shoulders.* Adrian, *dropping the books, holds up the fish, staring at it in stupefied awe.* Arthur *drops the flowers and joins him. The bell rings again.* Bella *picks up the flowers and thrusts them into* Arthur's *arms again, and pushes them both towards the garden door.*)

Adrian. Twenty pounds if it's an ounce !
Arthur. Nowhere near.
Adrian. I'll bet you——
Arthur. Don't you dare !

They are thrust out of the door, which Bella *locks after them as—*
The Curtain *falls.*

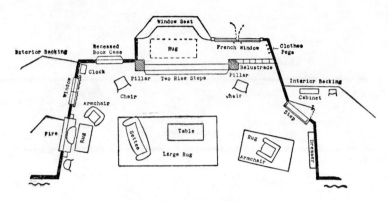

FURNITURE PLOT

Down Stage.—1 armchair and cushion L.
   1 rug L.
   1 Dutch dresser L.

Up Stage.—1 old linen or paper press L.
   1 occasional chair below the pillar L.
   Rack of clothes pegs L.
   1 window seat C.
   2 cushions on window seat C.
   1 rug below window seat on rostrum C.
   1 small table (next to pillar R.).
   1 occasional chair below the pillar R.
   1 recess bookcase with books R.
   1 grandfather clock R.
1 small magazine or paper rack, below window R.
1 armchair and cushion above fireplace R.
1 rug in front of fire R.
1 small armchair (preferably wood), below fire R.
Settee and 3 cushions, facing fire, ½ C.
Table set behind settee, ½ C.
1 large rug covering C. stage.
1 small covered chair on rostrum, L. up stage.

Curtains.—2 long curtains for french windows.
   4 small curtains for bay window.
   2 small curtains for window R.
Pelmets for all windows.

Off Stage in Door L.—2 dining-room chairs and 1 cabinet and 1 rug.

On Dresser.—Pewter plates, jugs and old gay-coloured plates on dresser down stage L.

On Mantelpiece.—1 small bird, bottle of sweets and any odd dressing to suit a cottage.

In Window R.—An ornament, a book and a tall old-fashioned bottle.

On Table up stage on Rostrum (below window-seat).—Old-patterned fruit plate.

Above Recess Bookcase.—An old-fashioned gun.

Above Grandfather Clock.—A large vase.

Above Clothes Rack.—A tennis racket.

On Pegs.—Several coats.

Pictures.—1 above dresser down stage L.
1 above linen press up stage L.
1 above small table on rostrum.
1 large picture above window R.
1 small picture above grandfather clock.
1 average size picture above fireplace.
1 on wall above chair down stage of fire.
1 china plate below picture down stage of fire.

PROPERTY LIST

ACT I

ON STAGE.

1 wastepaper basket.
1 " Mind the Step " printed on cardboard.
1 calendar for wall.
1 wooden coal bucket.

On Mantelpiece.—1 clock.
1 small mirror.
1 photograph of child in frame.
1 pen.
1 pipe.
1 pair of scissors.
1 box of matches.
1 cigarette box.
1 dressing-gown, set on hook of clothes peg up stage L.

On Sideboard.—6 small plates, 1 crumb-brush, pan, water jug and glass

In Sideboard Drawer.—6 knives and forks.

In Downstage Sideboard Drawer.—1 dozen jam-jar covers.

In Sideboard Cupboard.—1 tin cake-box, 1 jam spoon and jar of jam.

On Window Seat.—1 small wallet.

Set under downstage Cushion on Settee.—1 pair plimsols.

On Fireplace.—1 set of fire-irons (companion).
1 poker and 1 bellows.
1 drawing-book and pencil.
1 ordinary book.

ACT II, SCENE 1.

On Table C.—1 tin box containing fisherman's flies and casts
1 saucer with 3 casts.
2 fishing-fly books containing flies.
Golf club and newspaper.
1 magnifying glass.

On Chair above Fire.—1 cookery book.

On Armchair below Fire.—Magazine.

On Window Seat up stage.—Magazine.

Set 1 dressing-gown on hook by garden door.

ACT II, Scene 2.

Quick Change.

Strike off Table.—Pie, 2 prop. tomatoes, poison bottle.
Close all curtains.

Bring on Sideboard.—Tray with whisky, syphon and 4 glasses.
Stand poker upright in fireplace and leave sugar bowl and spoon on table.

ACT III

" *Times* " crossword on settee and pamphlets.

On Table c.—6 cups, saucers, spoons, sugar bowl, tea pot, cream jug and
    large tray and table cloth.

Set on table, cake tin, jam and cake in box, also jam spoon.

.

PERSONAL PROPERTY LIST

ACT I

Off Stage L.

MILDRED.—6 chip baskets, 1 handbag.

ARTHUR.—6 assorted parcels, a carrier bag containing parcels, 1 cake
    carton with ginger cake, 1 haversack, 1 fishing basket, 1 salmon-
    fishing rod.

MARCIA BRENT.—1 Jap. basket strapped, containing 1 prop. ham, half
    wrapped in greaseproof paper and 1 telegram.

MILDRED.—1 flower vase (empty), bundle of string.

SALLY SPENDER.—Bag of prop. tomatoes.

DENYS ROYD.—1 folded tent, strapped.

JIM BRENT.—Golf bag and clubs and tourist pamphlets.

ELLA SPENDER.—Shopping basket with parcels and containing small script.

BELLA HITCHINS.—1 paraffin can.

ARTHUR.—Bundle of small twigs, 3 fishing casts and saucer, pipe and pouch.

ADRIAN BARASFORD.—1 small tin of flies.

SAM PECKER.—1 scuttle of coke.

MARY JARROW.—1 parcel of lettuce.

Off Stage R.

SAM PECKER.—1 basket containing 12 potatoes, 1 prop. coin.

ACT II, Scene 1

Off Stage L

MILDRED.—Salad in bowl, cream jug, bundle of parsley.

MIRANDA.—1 basket of blackberries.

BELLA HITCHINS.—1 prop. pork pie on plate.

ELLA SPENDER.—1 counterpane.

ROWENA MARRIOT.—1 prop. letter.

MIRANDA.—Salt, pepper, cheese and butter on plates

BELLA HITCHINS.—Tablecloth.

MIRANDA.—1 poison bottle.

JIM BRENT.—1 set of snaps.

ROWENA.—1 mackintosh broken down.

MIRANDA.—1 pair of slippers.

ACT II, Scene 2.

Off Stage l.

ROWENA.—1 eiderdown and sheet.
DENYS ROYD.—1 kettle of hot water.
ADRIAN BARASFORD.—2 prop. pound notes (wet).

ACT III

Off Stage l.

MILDRED.—6 books, prop. jam in saucer and a piece of string, 1 Jap. basket opened) and straps, 1 dozen prop. eggs.
BELLA HITCHINS.—1 prop. salmon weighing 12 lbs., 1 letter (taken from script) attached to salmon, 2 parcels.
ELLA SPENDER.—Counterpane, doubled, from Act II.
MIRANDA.—Tent and strap for same.

Off Stage r.

MILDRED.—String bag for cabbages.
Set 4 prop. cabbages.

Off Stage l.

MILDRED.—Eggs in basket wrapped in newspaper, potatoes in basket, 1 plate with finished meal on, dish of plums.
DENYS ROYD.—1 suitcase.

PERSONAL HAND PROPS

DENYS ROYD.—Pouch, pipe, matches.
ARTHUR.—Pipe, pouch, matches.
ADRIAN BARASFORD.—1 small tin for flies, 1 small bottle for oil.
MILDRED.—1 handbag containing glasses, pencil and small notebook.
MIRANDA.—Gum boots and mackintosh broken down.
SAM PECKER.—1 prop. coin.
MARY.—1 handbag.
ROWENA.—1 handbag and gloves.
ELLA SPENDER.—1 handbag and gloves.
JIM BRENT.—6 snaps of child.

LIGHTING PLOT

This play can be lit by spot batten, float, back batten and perches, or, more simply, by float and battens with or without the addition of perches. In either case, the further assistance of F.O.H. lighting may be employed if the other lighting makes this necessary.

The lighting plot given below is on the basis of the ordinary float and battens, with perches.

There should, of course, be such floods on the exterior cloth as the size of stage requires.

The float and battens should have pink, white and amber circuits, and, if possible, separate use of the C., L. and R. sections of each.

The fire, and additional red fire spot is needed.

ACT I

To Open.—Float and Nos. 1 and 2 battens, amber, pink and white, FULL
No. 3 batten, white and amber only, FULL.
Straw and open white floods on exterior.
Straw length in interior backing L.
Ditto, if available, behind pillars, on bay.

FIRE CUES.—Fire OFF for this act, to open.   Smoke ON before CURTAIN up, and OFF as CURTAIN rises.

Cue 1.—DENYS.   " I am going to Hollywood."—Fire flicker ON.

Cue 2.—ADRIAN *enters* (1*st* time).—Fire flicker OFF.

Cue 3.—MILDRED.   " Come in, I'm in the sitting-room."—Fire flicker ON.

Cue 4.—ROWENA.   " The roads in America are wonderful."—Fire flicker OFF.

(Plug up flash box.)

Cue 5.—BELLA.   " Well, here goes . . ." (*She throws paraffin on the fire.*)- On 2nd throw : FLASH ON.   SMOKE.

ACT II, SCENE 1

To Open.—Float : all circuits at ¼.
 Battens : all circuits FULL
 Exterior floods ½.
 Lengths as before.
 FIRE ON—not spot.

Cue 1.—*Three minutes after* CURTAIN *up.*—All interior lighting up to FULL.

Cue 2.—ADRIAN.   " Your house has no bathroom."—Exterior floods to ½.

Cue 3.—MARY.   " Look, the sun is actually trying to shine."—All exterior lighting to FULL.

ACT II, SCENE 2

To Open.—Everything OUT, except fire and fire spot and No. 32 blue flood on exterior cloth.

Cue 1.—ROWENA.   " You were exceedingly rude."—Bring in pink only in float to ¼, and L. and R. section of No. 1 Batten to FULL.   Ditto in No. 2 Batten to ½, and L. perch on mantel. (Perches and battens on the word " *rude*," when oil lamp on mantel is lit.)

Cue 2.—*When masthead lamp is lit on* L. *pillar.*—Bring in C. section of No. 1 Batten to FULL.   Ditto of No. 2 Batten to ½.

(NOTE.—Fire and fire spot ON throughout.   The spot takes in the armchair above the fire, the garden door, and the L. pillar.)

ACT III

Lighting as for Act I.   All FULL UP.
Fire ON, but no spot.
Fire must be OUT *before* the concerted scene starts prior to the final CURTAIN.

MADE AND PRINTED IN GREAT BRITAIN BY
BUTLER & TANNER LTD, FROME AND LONDON

MADE IN ENGLAND